THRIVING IN A HOSTILE WORK ENVIRONMENT

Strategies for Resilience, Advocacy, and Positive Change

Victor Olewunne

Vista Press

Vista press
& Distribution Logistics Ltd.

*To all workers who dare to uphold their right
and push for positive changes in the work place,
this is a special tool for you. Your bravery is
guaranteed to make the world a better place.*

*Toxic people will pollute
everything around them.
Don't hesitate.
Fumigate.*

MANDY HALE

PREFACE

More Than Just Survival

Work is often more than just a job. For many, it's an integral part of our identity, a community, and a space where we hope to grow and flourish. But what happens when this environment turns toxic, when it feels more like a battlefield than a place of productivity and collaboration? Suddenly, the standard advice about "being a team player" or "keeping your head down and working hard" seems inadequate, even naive.

The harsh reality is that hostile work environments exist. Whether marked by overt harassment, subtle discrimination, or the constant drumbeat of belittling remarks and impossible expectations, these settings pose a threat not just to our career prospects, but also to our physical and mental well-being. The silence around this topic, often maintained due to fear of reprisals or a sense of helplessness, only exacerbates the problem.

This book, "Thriving in a Hostile Work Environment," aims to break that silence.

Why This Book Is Necessary

While there are countless professional development books on improving leadership, scaling the career ladder, and enhancing productivity, there is a notable dearth of comprehensive resources designed to help individuals navigate toxic workplaces. Some might argue that if the work environment is hostile, the only solution is to leave. While this is an option—and sometimes the only viable one—it's not always immediately feasible due to various personal and professional constraints.

It's for those who find themselves in this difficult position—caught between the proverbial rock and a hard place—that this book was written. We will explore ways you can protect your well-being, uphold your dignity, and even flourish despite the adversity you face. Because sometimes, survival isn't enough; you deserve to thrive.

What to Expect

The book is divided into four main sections. The first helps you identify what constitutes a hostile work environment, allowing for a better understanding of the problem. The second section focuses on self-care and coping strategies that help you maintain emotional and mental well-being. The third part offers guidance on navigating the system, from HR protocols to legal options. The final section discusses proactive strategies for shaping company culture and preparing for future steps, including the possibility of exiting your current job gracefully.

Who This Book Is For

This book is for anyone who has faced, is facing, or may face a toxic work environment. It's for those who have felt silenced, marginalized, or demeaned in their professional lives and are seeking actionable steps to reclaim their dignity and well-being. It is also for HR professionals, managers, and organizational leaders who are committed to creating and maintaining a culture that fosters inclusivity and respect.

Final Thoughts

"Thriving in a Hostile Work Environment" aims to be more than just a survival guide; it strives to be a resource that empowers you to take control of your professional life. My hope is that by the time you close the last page of this book, you will have gained the tools, confidence, and resources to navigate your challenging circumstances effectively and emerge not just unscathed, but stronger.

Here's to thriving, not just surviving.

With best wishes,

Victor Olewunne MPE

INTRODUCTION

Why We Need to Address
Hostile Work Environments

If work were just about clocking in, doing your job, and clocking out, a hostile work environment wouldn't be such a significant issue. However, the workplace is far more than just a venue for labor; it's a social ecosystem, a locus of personal and professional development, and often a defining aspect of our identities. When toxicity infiltrates this environment, the consequences can be severe, not just for individual employees but also for the organization as a whole.

Understanding the urgency of addressing hostile work environments is crucial for both employers and employees. Ignoring or trivializing the problem can lead to detrimental effects on mental health, productivity, and overall well-being. Here we delve into why it is imperative to tackle the issue head-on.

The Human Toll

Emotional and Psychological Impact

Workplace hostility can take a considerable emotional and psychological toll on employees. Symptoms can range from generalized anxiety and depression to severe forms of stress disorders. These mental health challenges can, in turn, affect an individual's overall quality of life, including relationships and physical well-being.

Physical Health Consequences

Chronic stress, a common result of enduring a hostile work environment, can lead to numerous health issues such as hypertension, digestive problems, and weakened immune systems. The body's constant "fight or flight" response can lead to long-term physical ailments that can have serious repercussions.

Impact on Career Growth

A toxic work environment can significantly hamper an individual's career trajectory. Employees might avoid taking on new responsibilities or challenging projects for fear of increased scrutiny or failure, which in the long run, limits opportunities for career growth and skill development.

Financial Costs to Organizations

Decreased Productivity
When employees are preoccupied with navigating a hostile environment, their focus shifts from

productivity and innovation to self-preservation. Tasks take longer to complete, and the quality of work suffers.

Increased Turnover

High attrition rates are a common outcome of a toxic workplace. The cost of recruiting, training, and onboarding new employees is substantial, often far outweighing the investment needed to cultivate a healthy work environment.

Legal Consequences

Ignoring signs of a hostile work environment can lead to legal challenges for an organization, including lawsuits related to harassment, discrimination, and wrongful termination. The financial ramifications, in this case, can be crippling, and the damage to the company's reputation can be long-lasting.

A Barrier to Diversity and Inclusion

A hostile work environment is often particularly detrimental to minority groups, including women, people of color, LGBTQ+ individuals, and those with disabilities. When these employees face additional barriers due to hostility or discrimination, it undermines any diversity and inclusion efforts the organization may be attempting.

The Ripple Effect on Society

Workplace hostility doesn't exist in a vacuum; it

has a ripple effect that extends into the broader society. Unhappy employees contribute less to their communities and may even perpetuate toxicity in other aspects of their lives, including in their families and social circles.

Addressing hostile work environments isn't just an HR issue—it's a human issue and a business imperative. The costs are too high, both in human and financial terms, to ignore the problem or hope it goes away on its own. Whether you're an employee suffering in a toxic work environment or an employer striving to create a more positive workspace, understanding the necessity of tackling this issue is the first step toward meaningful change.

Through acknowledgment, awareness, and proactive intervention, we can transform the workplace from a source of stress and strife to one of productivity, respect, and overall well-being. It's not just about avoiding negative outcomes but about fostering an environment where everyone can thrive.

Scope and Structure of the Book

Before diving into the complexities of navigating a hostile work environment, it's crucial to understand what this book aims to cover and how it's structured to guide you. This chapter outlines the scope of the book, explaining the topics that will be addressed, and the intended audience. It also describes the book's structure, so you can navigate through the chapters effectively to find the solutions that are most relevant to your situation.

Scope of the Book

<u>Topics Covered</u>

Identifying a Hostile Work Environment: Recognize the signs, symptoms, and dynamics that define a toxic workplace.

Emotional and Mental Well-being: Strategies for maintaining your emotional equilibrium in the face of workplace hostility.

Documenting and Reporting: Learn how to properly document incidents and when and how to escalate issues to HR or higher management.

Legal Framework: Understand the laws and regulations that protect employees from hostile work conditions, and when to consider legal action.

Organizational Culture: Unpack how culture contributes to hostility and explore strategies for becoming an agent of positive change within your organization.

Exit Strategies: Planning a graceful and strategic exit when leaving becomes the best or only option.

Intended Audience

This book is written with a broad audience in mind:

Employees: Individuals who are currently facing or have faced a hostile work environment.

HR Professionals: Those responsible for maintaining a healthy work environment and handling employee grievances.

Managers and Leaders: Anyone in a position of power who has the capability to influence workplace culture.

Job Seekers: Individuals looking to understand red flags in potential workplaces.

General Readers: Anyone interested in understanding the dynamics of workplace culture and psychology.

Structure of the Book

The book is divided into four main parts, each consisting of multiple chapters aimed at tackling the issue of hostile work environments from various angles.

Part I: Identifying the Problem

Aimed at helping you recognize and understand the elements that make up a hostile work environment.

Part II: Self-Care and Coping Strategies

Focuses on how you can protect yourself emotionally and mentally.

Part III: Navigating the System

A guide to taking appropriate actions, from filing reports to engaging with legal procedures.

Part IV: Proactive Strategies

Strategies for affecting organizational change and preparing for future steps, including potential exit strategies.

Each part is designed to be self-contained, so you can choose to read the book cover to cover or jump to sections that are most relevant to your situation.

Conclusion

Understanding the scope and structure of this book will help you make the most of the information, tools, and strategies it provides. Whether you're dealing with subtle hostility or overt harassment, this book aims to empower you with the knowledge and skills to not just survive but to thrive in challenging workplace conditions.

Next, we will delve into the unsettling but crucial topic of recognizing a hostile work environment. This understanding is the first step toward reclaiming your professional life and personal peace. Let's get started.

PROLOGUE

The Moment of Realization

Imagine walking into your office, your heart pounding with a sense of dread. The walls seem to close in as you take your seat, already anticipating the next snide remark or blatant act of exclusion. You wonder how a place that once held promise could now be the source of such anxiety and frustration.

For many of us, that moment of realization—that we are entrenched in a hostile work environment —is jarring. The workplace, a place where we spend a significant portion of our lives, becomes a battleground where survival instincts take over. The dream of fulfilling job roles, advancing in our careers, or simply enjoying our day-to-day work becomes a distant, unreachable star.

As you hold this book in your hands, you may be experiencing a range of emotions: fear, anger, despair, or even a sense of vindication that someone is finally acknowledging what you've been going through. You are not alone. The purpose of this book is to arm you with the tools, strategies, and wisdom to confront the hostility that casts a shadow over your professional life.

Stories that Need to Be Told

Throughout the book, you will find real-life stories and examples—situations that are, unfortunately, all too common yet seldom discussed openly. Some names and identifying details have been changed to protect privacy, but the essence of each experience remains true. These stories serve as both cautionary tales and sources of inspiration, showing us how individuals have navigated, combated, and often transcended the toxicity in their workplaces.

Beyond Buzzwords

In an era where terms like "workplace culture," "inclusivity," and "employee well-being" are buzzwords that adorn corporate mission statements and HR pamphlets, the stark reality is that many organizations are still struggling to convert these ideals into practice. This book is designed to cut through the jargon and offer pragmatic advice, because buzzwords won't protect you from a bullying boss or a discriminatory colleague—but effective strategies can.

Action Over Despair

A hostile work environment can induce a sense of

paralysis, making us feel trapped and powerless. One of the key objectives of this book is to help you move from a state of despair to one of action. By understanding your rights, examining your options, and strategizing your moves, you can transition from being a victim to becoming an advocate—for yourself and for others who may be facing similar situations.

Your Journey to Thriving

"Thriving in a Hostile Work Environment" is more than just a book; it's a companion for a journey no one should have to take alone. Whether you're skimming through it to find immediate answers to pressing issues, or reading it cover to cover for a holistic understanding, consider this book a resource that you can return to time and again.

You deserve better than to merely survive your workdays. You deserve to thrive, to reclaim your professional joy and personal peace. And it's my earnest hope that this book will help guide you towards that goal.

Let's begin.

PART I:
IDENTIFYING
THE PROBLEM

CHAPTER 1

Recognizing a Hostile
Work Environment

Welcome to one of the most critical chapters of this book: recognizing a hostile work environment. While you might think that hostile actions or behaviors would be glaringly obvious, the reality is often much subtler. A hostile work environment can manifest itself in a variety of ways—from overt acts of discrimination and harassment to more covert actions like constant undermining, backstabbing, or sidelining.

In this chapter, we will unpack the concept of a hostile work environment in detail to provide you with a nuanced understanding of what it entails. We will delve into the various types and forms of hostility that you might encounter, as well as the telltale signs and red flags that should alert you to problematic dynamics in the workplace. The aim is not only to equip you with the knowledge to recognize hostility but also to empower you to differentiate between an actual hostile environment and occasional stress or disagreements that can occur in any workplace.

Why is this recognition so crucial? Simply put, you can't address a problem if you can't identify it. And the longer these issues persist, the more detrimental they can be to your well-being, productivity, and overall career trajectory. Understanding the signs is the first step towards taking proactive measures to either resolve the issue or protect yourself effectively.

In a world where the line between work and life continues to blur, and where we often spend more time with colleagues than loved ones, being in a hostile work environment can have far-reaching implications for both your mental and physical health. By learning to recognize the signs early, you have the chance to take action before the situation escalates, thereby safeguarding not just your job but your overall quality of life.

Stay tuned as we take a deep dive into this complex, often murky, yet incredibly vital topic.

Types of Hostility: Overt and Covert

Recognizing the existence of a hostile work environment is the first step toward navigating it effectively. However, hostility in the workplace can manifest in various forms—some obvious and some subtle. It's crucial to differentiate between overt and covert types of hostility to adequately address the situation and plan your strategy. This chapter aims to break down these two broad categories to help you identify the specific challenges you may be facing.

Overt Hostility

Definition

Overt hostility refers to explicit, easily observable behaviors that create an unpleasant, intimidating, or exclusionary workplace. These actions are generally blatant and unmistakable.

Examples

Verbal Harassment: Frequent derogatory comments, racial slurs, or sexual innuendos.

Physical Intimidation: Acts of physical violence or threats that create an atmosphere of fear.

Explicit Discrimination: Openly discriminating against employees based on gender, race, sexual orientation, religion, or other protected categories.

Bullying: Repeated aggressive behaviors intended to belittle, demean, or intimidate others.

Impact

Overt hostility can lead to immediate and severe emotional distress. It often results in diminished self-esteem, increased stress levels, and can negatively impact job performance. The long-term psychological and physical consequences can be significant.

Reporting and Legal Recourse

Because overt acts are more easily documented and witnessed, there are often clearer paths for reporting these behaviors through HR or other organizational channels. Legal recourse is also more straightforward, though not guaranteed to be successful.

Covert Hostility

Definition

Covert hostility refers to implicit, less easily observable behaviors that contribute to a hostile work environment. These actions are insidious, often disguised as "normal" workplace interactions, making them harder to identify and prove.

Examples

Microaggressions: Subtle comments or actions that marginalize individuals based on their gender, race, or other protected characteristics.

Gaslighting: Manipulating someone into questioning their reality or sanity, often used to deflect responsibility for hostile behavior.

Exclusion: Intentionally leaving someone out of meetings, conversations, or workplace social events, isolating them from their colleagues.

Workplace Sabotage: Undermining someone's work

performance subtly, such as withholding necessary information or assigning impossible deadlines.

Impact

Covert hostility can have long-term detrimental effects on an employee's mental health, self-esteem, and career progress. Because it's less obvious, it can take longer to recognize, making it a breeding ground for chronic stress and anxiety.

Reporting and Legal Recourse

Covert hostility is more challenging to prove and report because it often lacks hard evidence. However, documentation and witness testimonies can sometimes provide sufficient grounds for action, whether through HR or, in extreme cases, legal intervention.

Understanding the different forms of workplace hostility—both overt and covert—is essential for effectively navigating a hostile work environment. Recognizing these behaviors for what they are can empower you to take appropriate action, whether that involves reporting the behavior, seeking legal counsel, or implementing self-care strategies.

Signs and Red Flags

Recognizing a hostile work environment can sometimes be a nuanced and challenging task, especially when the hostility is covert or subtly ingrained in the company culture. Whether you're already part of an organization or are considering joining one, being aware of signs and red flags can make all the difference in identifying and addressing the issue. In this section we will discuss various indicators that should alert you to a potentially hostile work environment.

Signs of Overt Hostility

Verbal Abuse and Harassment

Openly derogatory comments, shouting, and insulting language aimed at belittling or intimidating others is a clear red flag.

Patterns of Discrimination

If you observe or experience repeated discriminatory actions or comments based on race, gender, sexual orientation, religion, or other protected characteristics, this is a significant red flag.

Physical Intimidation or Violence

Any signs of physical aggression or threats should be taken seriously. This type of behavior is not only hostile but potentially criminal.

Excessive Public Humiliation

Publicly belittling or demeaning employees is another sign of overt hostility and is often used as a power play to assert dominance.

Signs of Covert Hostility

Exclusion and Isolation

Being intentionally left out of meetings, communications, or social activities is a subtle but damaging form of workplace hostility.

Gaslighting and Manipulation

If your experiences are regularly invalidated, or you're made to question your own perceptions, you may be experiencing gaslighting.

Unequal Treatment

Patterns of unequal treatment, such as consistent lack of opportunities for advancement, unfair distribution of workload, or unexplained salary discrepancies, can indicate covert hostility.

Negative Gossip and Rumors

A workplace that thrives on gossip and backbiting can be subtly hostile, as rumors can severely damage reputations and sow discord among employees.

Organizational Red Flags

High Turnover Rates

A high level of employee turnover is often a sign of systemic issues, including a potentially hostile work environment.

Lack of Diversity

A monolithic employee base, especially in leadership

roles, can be a sign that the organization is not welcoming or inclusive.

Poor HR Practices

An unresponsive or dismissive HR department may indicate that complaints about hostility are unlikely to be addressed adequately.

Inadequate Training and Onboarding

Insufficient training for new hires, especially around organizational values and harassment policies, can be a red flag that hostility is not a priority issue for the organization.

Personal Indicators

Dreading Work

If you find yourself dreading going to work or feeling relieved when the workweek is over, this could be a sign that the environment is hostile or toxic.

Physical or Mental Health Issues

If you've experienced a sudden decline in your physical or mental health since joining a particular workplace, this is a significant indicator that the environment may be affecting you adversely.

Awareness is the first step toward navigating and addressing a hostile work environment. By recognizing these signs and red flags, you can assess the severity of the issue, decide on the best course of action, and determine whether or not the situation can be remedied or if it's best to seek opportunities elsewhere.

The Cost to Individuals and Organizations

The consequences of a hostile work environment extend far beyond the immediate unpleasantness of the office setting. Both individuals and organizations bear significant costs that can have long-lasting effects on personal well-being and business success. This chapter aims to elucidate the multi-faceted toll that hostility takes on various stakeholders.

Cost to Individuals

Emotional and Psychological Well-being

The mental toll of working in a hostile environment can be immense, leading to anxiety, depression, and other mental health issues. These conditions can affect not only your job performance but also your personal life, relationships, and overall happiness.

Physical Health

Chronic stress is a common outcome of a hostile work environment, leading to various health issues such as hypertension, digestive disorders, and a compromised immune system. Over time, these can evolve into more severe health conditions, including heart disease and chronic gastrointestinal issues.

Career Progression

Hostile work environments often lead to reduced productivity and enthusiasm for taking on new tasks or challenges. This can result in stunted career growth, limiting opportunities for advancement, skill development, and wage increases.

Financial Costs

Medical bills for treating stress-related illnesses, the cost of job hunting, or even legal fees for harassment cases can add up, putting an additional financial burden on the individual.

Cost to Organizations

Decreased Productivity

Employees facing hostility are less likely to be engaged and productive. Projects take longer to complete, the quality of work suffers, and innovation is stifled.

High Turnover Rates

The costs of employee turnover can be staggering, including the expenses for recruiting, onboarding, and training new staff. High attrition rates are usually a sign of deeper organizational issues that can perpetuate the hostile environment.

Legal Risks

Companies risk facing lawsuits for failing to address

issues related to harassment, discrimination, and creating or permitting a hostile work environment. Legal battles can be expensive, time-consuming, and damaging to the company's reputation.

Damage to Company Reputation

Word of mouth, online reviews on employment websites, and even media coverage can severely damage a company's reputation, making it harder to attract top talent and retain clients.

Poor Team Dynamics

A hostile work environment can breed distrust, poor communication, and rivalry among team members. This compromises the collaborative spirit that is often vital for organizational success.

Impacts on Shareholder Value

The aggregate of these costs can eventually affect a company's bottom line and therefore its attractiveness to investors, which in the long term can result in a decline in shareholder value.

Broader Economic Impact

When one considers the aggregated effect of hostile work environments across multiple organizations, the economic impact becomes considerable. Loss of productivity, high turnover rates, and legal costs contribute to an inefficient labor market, reducing overall economic output.

In conclusion, understanding the extensive costs of a hostile work environment can help motivate both individuals and organizations to take the issue seriously. The repercussions are far-reaching, affecting every facet of both personal and professional life. By proactively addressing the issue, individuals can protect their well-being, and organizations can safeguard their reputation, financial health, and overall success.

Example of Discrimination in the Workplace

Meet Sarah, a talented graphic designer who has been with her company for several years. Sarah prides herself on her creativity and dedication to her work. However, over time, she begins to notice a pattern of behavior that makes her increasingly uncomfortable.

Recognizing the Signs:

Microaggressions: Sarah starts noticing subtle comments from her supervisor, Mark. He frequently makes remarks about her appearance and clothing choices that he never makes about her male colleagues. For example, he once commented, "Sarah, are you sure that outfit is appropriate for the office?"

Exclusion: Sarah notices that her colleagues are often invited to informal team gatherings after work, but she is consistently left out. This exclusion leaves her feeling isolated and undervalued.

Unequal Opportunities: Sarah observes that male colleagues with similar or even less experience receive promotions and challenging projects while she seems stuck in her current role.

Inappropriate Jokes: Mark occasionally makes jokes that Sarah finds offensive. He once told a sexist joke during a team meeting, which made her uncomfortable and silenced her.

Taking Action:

Documenting Incidents: Sarah begins to keep a detailed record of each incident, including dates, times, locations, and the names of any witnesses.

Seeking Advice: She confides in a trusted colleague, Emily, who suggests speaking with the HR department about the issue.

Reporting the Behavior: Sarah schedules a meeting with HR to discuss her concerns. She presents her documented evidence and explains how Mark's behavior is creating a hostile work environment for her.

Resolution:

Investigation: HR conducts a thorough investigation into Sarah's complaints, interviewing her, Mark, and witnesses. They also review her documentation.

Action Taken: After concluding the investigation, HR determines that Mark's behavior violated the company's anti-discrimination policies. Mark is given a formal warning and required to undergo sensitivity training.

Changes in the Workplace: The company takes steps to address the broader issue of gender discrimination in the workplace. They implement diversity training for all employees, revise their promotion process to ensure fairness, and create a more inclusive work environment.

Sarah's recognition of the signs of a hostile work environment and her willingness to take action led to positive changes in her workplace. While it was a challenging journey, her courage in reporting the discrimination not only improved her own situation but also contributed to a more inclusive and respectful workplace culture for everyone.

CHAPTER 2

The Players Involved

The Bully

T he term "bully" often conjures up images of school playgrounds, but unfortunately, bullying doesn't always end with adolescence. The workplace can serve as another arena where bullies operate, causing emotional and psychological harm to their targets. This chapter aims to delve into the profile of a workplace bully, the tactics they use, and the reasons behind their behavior. Understanding the bully can be the first step in devising effective strategies to counteract their harmful impact.

Characteristics of a Bully

Need for Control

A common trait among bullies is the need to control situations and people. This can manifest as micromanagement, authoritarian leadership styles, or manipulation.

Lack of Empathy

Bullies often demonstrate a lack of empathy, finding it easy to dismiss the feelings and well-being of others if it serves their goals.

Skill at Manipulation

Many bullies are adept at manipulating both situations and people. They know how to use the system to their advantage and can be charming when it suits them.

Insecurity

Despite a facade of confidence, many bullies are driven by deep-seated insecurities. Their bullying behavior can be a coping mechanism to mask their own feelings of inadequacy.

Tactics Employed by Bullies

Verbal Abuse

This includes shouting, name-calling, and humiliation, often in front of colleagues to assert dominance and degrade the victim.

Exclusion and Isolation

Bullies may intentionally leave you out of important meetings, communications, or social events to make you feel marginalized.

Undermining

This can manifest as subtle or overt acts aimed at sabotaging your work, credibility, or relationships within the workplace.

Gaslighting

Bullies often use gaslighting to manipulate you into doubting your own experiences or judgments, making it easier for them to maintain control.

Why Do They Do It?

Personal Insecurity

As mentioned earlier, bullying often stems from the bully's own insecurities. Targeting others can make them feel more secure or superior.

Cultural Factors

Sometimes, the organizational culture may inadvertently support bullying by rewarding aggressive, cutthroat behavior, or by failing to enforce anti-bullying policies.

Lack of Consequences

In some workplaces, there is a lack of adequate mechanisms to report and address bullying, allowing the behavior to continue without repercussions.

How to Protect Yourself

Documentation: Keep a detailed record of every

incident, including dates, times, places, people involved, and the nature of the bullying.

Seek Support: Speak with trusted colleagues or friends about the situation. They may offer valuable perspectives and emotional support.

Report: Utilize your company's grievance procedures or go to HR with your documentation.

Legal Advice: In extreme cases, consider seeking legal advice to understand your rights and options.

Self-Care: Take steps to maintain your physical and mental health, such as exercise, relaxation techniques, or consulting a mental health professional.

Understanding the bully's characteristics, tactics, and motivations can empower you to take control of the situation and minimize their impact on your well-being. While it's challenging to change a bully's behavior, you can take steps to protect yourself and seek avenues for redress.

The Enablers

While much attention is focused on the bully, there's another group that plays a significant but often overlooked role in perpetuating a hostile work environment: the enablers. These individuals may not engage in the overtly destructive behaviors of the bully, but their actions—or lack thereof—can create a culture that allows hostility to persist. Understanding the dynamics of enabling is crucial for effectively addressing and dismantling a toxic work environment.

Characteristics of Enablers

Fearful

Many enablers operate out of fear—fear of retaliation, of being the next target, or of risking their job security.

Ignorant or Unaware

Some enablers may be genuinely ignorant of the harm being done, either due to a lack of emotional intelligence or because they have been manipulated into thinking the behavior is acceptable.

Self-Interested

In some cases, enablers benefit from the bully's actions, either by gaining favor, avoiding additional work, or being part of an "inner circle."

Apathetic

A lack of empathy or moral concern can also characterize enablers. They may be indifferent to the harm caused as long as it does not affect them personally.

Types of Enabling Behavior

Silence

Failing to speak up against wrongful actions is one of the most common forms of enabling. Silence can be taken as agreement, emboldening the bully.

Justification
Some enablers defend or justify the bully's actions, often painting them as a strong leader who is merely "tough but fair," thereby normalizing the toxic behavior.

Collaboration
Active participation in the bully's tactics, such as spreading rumors or isolating a target, moves the enabler from a passive to an active role in the hostile environment.

Victim-Blaming
In some cases, enablers may blame the victim for "provoking" the bully or for being "too sensitive," thereby deflecting accountability away from the bully.

The Cost of Enabling

Compounding Harm
The presence of enablers can compound the emotional and psychological harm experienced by the target, creating a sense of isolation and helplessness.

Culture of Hostility
When enabling behavior is pervasive, it contributes to a toxic organizational culture where hostility can thrive unchecked.

Legal Ramifications

Enablers, especially those in managerial positions, can also be held liable in cases where the hostile work environment leads to legal action.

Strategies for Addressing Enablers

Open Dialogue
Attempt to have an open conversation with the enabler to make them aware of the impact of their actions.

Reporting
Document instances of enabling behavior alongside bullying incidents when reporting to HR or higher management.

Building Alliances
Find allies within the organization who are also concerned about the toxic environment and are willing to stand against both bullies and enablers.

External Consultation
In extreme cases, legal advice or third-party mediation might be necessary to address the behavior of enablers effectively.

Enablers play a crucial but often unnoticed role in sustaining a hostile work environment. By recognizing and understanding the characteristics and tactics of enablers, you can develop strategies to confront and neutralize their impact. Effective change not only involves dealing with the bullies but also addressing the enablers who make it easier for toxic behavior to persist.

The Targets

In a hostile work environment, the most visibly impacted individuals are the targets. Understanding who these targets are, the reasons they may be selected, and the unique challenges they face is crucial for both intervention and prevention. This section aims to demystify the profile of a target, shed light on the psychological impact of being targeted, and offer coping strategies to help individuals regain a sense of control and well-being.

Characteristics of Targets

High Competence
Ironically, targets often have a high level of competence, posing a perceived threat to the bully or others who may feel insecure.

Ethical and Honest
Individuals with strong ethical convictions and a commitment to honesty may be targeted as they may be less likely to go along with unethical or questionable activities.

Non-Confrontational
Targets often have a non-confrontational nature and may be conflict-averse, which makes them easier to manipulate or intimidate.

Vulnerable
Some targets may be singled out based on

characteristics that mark them as socially or culturally vulnerable, such as gender, ethnicity, or age.

Psychological Impact on Targets

Emotional Toll
Being a target can lead to a range of emotional impacts, from heightened stress and anxiety to severe depression.

Loss of Self-Esteem
Persistent targeting can erode self-esteem, leading to self-doubt and affecting not just work performance but overall well-being.

Trust Issues
Continuous targeting can make it difficult for the individual to trust colleagues and may even impair their ability to form professional relationships in the future.

Coping Strategies for Targets

Documenting Incidents
Maintain a detailed log of incidents, noting dates, times, individuals involved, and the nature of each event.

Seek Support Networks
Reach out to friends, family, or even professional counselors to discuss your experiences and emotional state.

Reporting
Use the established procedures within your organization to report the harassment. Always back your case with the documentation you've collected.

Self-Care
Engage in activities that help you recharge emotionally and physically. Exercise, meditation, and time spent on hobbies can be helpful.

Know When to Exit
Sometimes, the best option may be to leave the hostile environment. While not an admission of defeat, recognizing when to exit can sometimes be the most empowering decision.

How Organizations Can Protect Targets

Clear Anti-Harassment Policies: Organizations must have clearly stated policies against all forms of harassment.

Training and Awareness: Regular training sessions can educate employees on the consequences of harassment and how to report it.

Accessible Reporting Channels: Easy, confidential methods for reporting harassment should be established.

Prompt Action: Organizations must take timely action on any reports of harassment to protect the target and deter the perpetrators.

Being a target in a hostile work environment is an emotionally and psychologically draining experience. By understanding the characteristics and challenges unique to targets, we can develop a comprehensive set of coping strategies. Equally important is organizational involvement in protecting targets by creating a culture that does not tolerate harassment in any form.

The Bystanders

Bystanders occupy a unique position in the dynamics of a hostile work environment. They are neither the perpetrators nor the direct targets, but their role can be surprisingly influential. Understanding the psychology, challenges, and potential of bystanders can offer additional avenues for addressing toxicity in the workplace.

Characteristics of Bystanders

Moral Ambiguity
Bystanders often find themselves in morally ambiguous situations, uncertain of how to act or intervene.

Risk Aversion
The fear of becoming a target themselves, facing professional repercussions, or disturbing the status quo can deter bystanders from taking action.

Ignorance or Minimization
Some bystanders may be unaware of the seriousness of the issue or may minimize its impact, believing it to

be a "normal" part of workplace dynamics.

Social Pressure
The influence of a group or organizational culture can also sway bystanders, either encouraging them to intervene or discouraging them from acting.

The Bystander Effect

The phenomenon where the presence of others discourages an individual from intervening in an emergency situation is known as the "bystander effect." In a work environment, this can manifest as an unspoken collective decision to ignore or tolerate hostile behavior.

Roles Bystanders Can Play

The Observer
Simply bears witness to the incidents but takes no action.

The Silent Supporter
Offers quiet emotional support to the target but does not take any public action.

The Intervener
Takes active steps to intervene, either by confronting the bully, supporting the target openly, or reporting the incidents.

The Advocate
Goes beyond the immediate situation to advocate for systemic changes in the workplace that prevent

future incidents.

Strategies for Empowering Bystanders

Education and Training
Workshops on the impact of hostility and the importance of bystander intervention can equip employees with the tools they need to act.

Anonymity and Reporting
Offering anonymous reporting channels can reduce the perceived risk of intervening.

Leadership Endorsement
Explicit endorsement and support from leadership can empower bystanders to take action.

Encourage Team Responsibility
Promote a culture where everyone feels responsible for maintaining a respectful and inclusive environment.

The Ripple Effect

Bystanders who take positive action not only assist the immediate target but also send a powerful message throughout the organization. This ripple effect can alter the culture, making it less hospitable to bullying and more conducive to cooperation and mutual respect.

Bystanders hold a considerable amount of untapped power in the dynamics of a hostile work environment. By understanding their challenges and potential, we can create strategies to empower them to take positive action. Their involvement can be pivotal, serving as a catalyst for transforming a toxic atmosphere into a more healthy, respectful, and productive one.

Historical Example: The Women of the Ford Dagenham Strike (1968)

In 1968, a group of women working at the Ford Motor Company's Dagenham plant in the United Kingdom found themselves in a hostile work environment due to significant disparities in pay and unequal treatment compared to their male counterparts. This historical event showcases the players involved in a hostile work environment and their fight for change.

The Players:

The Women Workers: The primary victims of the hostile work environment were the female machinists at the Ford Dagenham plant. They were responsible for sewing seat covers for the cars but were classified as unskilled workers and paid significantly less than the male employees performing similar work in other parts of the factory.

Ford Motor Company: The employer, Ford Motor Company, was a major player in creating the hostile work environment. The company's policies and practices, such as paying women less for the same work as men and maintaining a hierarchical and discriminatory workplace culture, contributed to the unfair treatment of female employees.

Trade Unions: Trade unions played a pivotal role in addressing the hostile work environment. The women workers were part of the National Union of Vehicle Builders (NUVB), and their leaders supported their fight for equal pay and recognition of their skills. However, the relationship between the unions and the female workers was sometimes strained due to gender biases within the unions themselves.

Political Leaders: Local and national political leaders also became key players in the struggle. Barbara Castle, the Secretary of State for Employment and Productivity in the UK government, got involved in the negotiations and helped mediate the dispute. Her support added political weight to the women's cause.

Public Opinion: Public opinion and the media played a significant role in raising awareness of the issue. The women's strike garnered widespread attention and sympathy from the public, which put additional pressure on Ford and the government to address the pay disparity.

Resolution:

The Ford Dagenham strike, led by the determined women machinists, ultimately resulted in significant changes:

- In 1970, the Equal Pay Act was passed in the UK, making it illegal to pay women less than men for the same work. This landmark legislation was a direct outcome of the strike.

- The strike also inspired broader discussions about gender equality and women's rights in the workplace, contributing to the feminist movement of the era.

- It served as a precursor to the broader labor and civil rights movements, highlighting the power of collective action and the importance of addressing hostile work environments.

This historical example illustrates how individuals, employers, trade unions, political leaders, and public opinion can all play crucial roles in addressing and rectifying a hostile work environment, ultimately leading to positive changes in workplace practices and policies.

CHAPTER 3

*Legal Framework and
Responsibilities*

Discrimination Laws and Their Relevance.

Understanding the legal landscape is crucial for anyone dealing with a hostile work environment. Discrimination laws provide a framework for identifying, addressing, and remedying workplace hostility based on certain protected characteristics. This chapter will outline key aspects of discrimination laws, their relevance to hostile work environments, and how they can be used as a tool for change.

Disclaimer: The information provided in this chapter is not legal advice. For legal advice tailored to your situation, consult a qualified attorney.

Federal Laws in the United States

Title VII of the Civil Rights Act of 1964

Title VII prohibits employers from discriminating based on race, color, religion, sex, or national origin. Sexual harassment is also considered a form of sex discrimination under Title VII.

Reference: U.S. Equal Employment Opportunity Commission (EEOC) - Title VII of the Civil Rights Act

The Americans with Disabilities Act (ADA)

This act prohibits discrimination against qualified individuals with disabilities in the job application process, hiring, advancement, termination, compensation, and other terms, conditions, and privileges of employment.

Reference: U.S. Department of Justice - Americans with Disabilities Act

Age Discrimination in Employment Act (ADEA)

The ADEA prohibits employment discrimination against persons 40 years of age or older.

Reference: U.S. Equal Employment Opportunity Commission (EEOC) - Age Discrimination

Other Laws

Other federal laws, such as the Pregnancy Discrimination Act and the Genetic Information Nondiscrimination Act, also protect against specific forms of workplace discrimination.

State Laws

Each state may have its own set of discrimination laws, often expanding upon federal laws to include additional protected categories such as sexual orientation, gender identity, and more.

Reference: Check your state's labor department or human rights commission website for details specific to your jurisdiction.

Other Country's Laws on Discrimination

Countries in Europe, Asia and Africa have similar anti-discrimination laws.

Discrimination Laws in the United Kingdom.

In the United Kingdom, discrimination laws are in place to protect individuals from unfair treatment based on various characteristics such as age, disability, gender, race, religion or belief, sexual orientation, and gender reassignment. These laws are essential for promoting equality and ensuring that everyone has the same opportunities and rights in various aspects of life, including the workplace. Discrimination laws in the UK are primarily governed by the Equality Act 2010.

Here is an overview of key aspects of discrimination laws in the UK:

The Equality Act 2010: The Equality Act 2010 is the primary piece of legislation that governs discrimination in the UK. It replaced previous anti-discrimination laws and provides comprehensive protection against various forms of discrimination.

Protected Characteristics: The Equality Act 2010 identifies several protected characteristics, which are personal attributes that individuals should not be discriminated against because of. These characteristics include:

- Age
- Disability
- Gender reassignment
- Marriage and civil partnership
- Pregnancy and maternity
- Race
- Religion or belief
- Sex
- Sexual orientation

Types of Discrimination

The Equality Act 2010 outlines different types of discrimination, including:

Direct Discrimination: Treating someone less favorably because of a protected characteristic.

Indirect Discrimination: Applying a policy, practice, or rule that has a disproportionately adverse impact on individuals with a particular protected characteristic.

Harassment: Unwanted behavior related to a protected characteristic that violates a person's dignity or creates an offensive, intimidating, hostile, or degrading environment.

Victimization: Treating someone unfairly because they have made a complaint or supported someone else's complaint about discrimination.

Workplace Discrimination: Discrimination in the workplace is prohibited under the Equality Act 2010. This covers all aspects of employment, including recruitment, terms and conditions, pay, promotions, training, and dismissals.

Reasonable Adjustments: Employers are required to make reasonable adjustments to accommodate the needs of disabled employees or job applicants. This can include providing accessible facilities or adjusting work hours.

Positive Action: In some cases, employers are allowed to take positive action to address underrepresentation or disadvantage faced by individuals with protected characteristics.

Enforcement: Individuals who believe they have experienced discrimination can bring a claim before an employment tribunal. Employers found guilty of discrimination may be required to pay compensation or take specific actions to rectify the situation.

Public Sector Equality Duty: Public authorities have

a duty to eliminate discrimination, advance equality of opportunity, and foster good relations between different groups.

Equality and Human Rights Commission (EHRC): The EHRC is responsible for promoting and enforcing equality and human rights laws in the UK. They provide guidance and support on discrimination issues.

It's important to note that discrimination laws in the UK are complex and subject to change. If you believe you have experienced discrimination or need guidance on discrimination laws, it is advisable to seek legal advice or contact the Equality and Human Rights Commission for assistance. Additionally, employers have a responsibility to be aware of and comply with these laws to create a fair and inclusive workplace for all employees.

Discrimination Laws in Nigeria

Discrimination laws in Nigeria, like in other places, are established to protect individuals from unfair treatment and ensure equal opportunities regardless of various personal characteristics. Nigeria has several laws and regulations in place to address discrimination, with a focus on promoting equality, human rights, and social justice. Here's an overview of discrimination laws in Nigeria:

The Constitution of Nigeria: The 1999 Constitution

of Nigeria, as amended, serves as the supreme law of the land and provides fundamental human rights and freedoms. It prohibits discrimination on the grounds of ethnicity, religion, sex, or political opinion. Section 42 of the Constitution explicitly prohibits discrimination in Nigeria.

The Discrimination Against Persons with Disabilities (Prohibition) Act: Enacted in 2018, this law aims to eliminate discrimination against persons with disabilities. It requires public and private organizations to provide reasonable accommodation and access to facilities for persons with disabilities.

Labor Laws: Nigerian labor laws, including the Labor Act and the Employees' Compensation Act, prohibit workplace discrimination based on race, gender, religion, disability, and other protected characteristics. Employers are required to provide equal employment opportunities and fair treatment for all employees.

The Criminal Code and Penal Code: These criminal laws address various forms of discrimination and hate crimes, such as hate speech, ethnic or religious violence, and incitement to discrimination or violence.

Gender Discrimination: Nigeria has laws specifically aimed at addressing gender discrimination, including the National Gender Policy and the Violence Against Persons (Prohibition) Act (2015). These laws are designed to protect women and girls from various forms of discrimination, including domestic violence and harmful traditional practices.

Religious Freedom: Nigeria is religiously diverse, and laws are in place to protect freedom of religion. Discrimination based on religion is prohibited, and individuals have the right to practice their faith without fear of discrimination.

Anti-Discrimination Agencies: Nigeria has agencies such as the National Human Rights Commission (NHRC) and the National Agency for the Prohibition of Trafficking in Persons (NAPTIP) that work to address and prevent various forms of discrimination, including human trafficking and gender-based violence.

International Conventions and Treaties: Nigeria is a signatory to international treaties and conventions that address discrimination, including the Convention on the Elimination of All Forms of Discrimination Against Women (CEDAW) and the International Convention on the Elimination of All Forms of Racial Discrimination (ICERD). These treaties provide additional legal frameworks to combat discrimination.

It's important to note that while these laws and regulations exist, the effective enforcement of anti-discrimination measures in Nigeria can be a challenge. Discrimination persists in various forms, and there is ongoing work to ensure that the laws are fully implemented and that discrimination is combated effectively.

Individuals who believe they have experienced discrimination in Nigeria should seek legal advice and consider reporting incidents to relevant authorities or human rights organizations. Promoting awareness of discrimination issues and advocating for equality and inclusion are essential steps toward addressing discrimination in Nigeria.

Legal Recourse

Filing a Complaint: The first step is often to file a complaint with the human resources department.

Reporting to Authorities: If internal channels fail to resolve the issue, you may file a charge with the EEOC or the equivalent state agency in US, or similar body in your own country.

Legal Action: If the government agency does not resolve the issue, you may have the option to file a lawsuit.

Importance of Documentation

Keeping a meticulous record of incidents can provide vital evidence should legal action become necessary.

Relevance to Hostile Work Environments

Discrimination laws are particularly relevant because they provide specific avenues for legal recourse for targets. Employers are also more likely to take action to prevent discrimination, in part due to the risk of legal repercussions.

Understanding discrimination laws is crucial for anyone navigating a hostile work environment. These laws serve not just as a tool for remediation but also as a deterrent against discriminatory practices in the first place. Make effort to be acquainted with the laws that apply in the country or location where you reside or work.

Harassment Policies - A Framework for Accountability

Harassment policies act as the backbone of an organization's stance against workplace hostility. Properly constructed and implemented, these policies serve as a road map for behavior, reporting mechanisms, and disciplinary actions. This section aims to explain the significance of robust harassment policies, what they should ideally contain, and how they influence the workplace atmosphere.

Why Harassment Policies are Crucial

Legal Shield
In many jurisdictions, having a clear and detailed harassment policy can protect an organization legally by showing due diligence in preventing harassment.

Behavioral Guide
A well-defined policy sets the tone for what behavior is acceptable and what is not, leaving no room for ambiguity.

Promotes Accountability
Having a policy in place provides a framework for handling complaints, conducting investigations, and implementing disciplinary actions, thereby promoting accountability.

Essential Components of Harassment Policies

Definition of Harassment
The policy should define what constitutes harassment, including both overt and covert actions, and it should cover all protected categories as outlined in relevant laws.

Reporting Mechanism
Detailed steps on how to report harassment should be laid out, including multiple avenues for reporting.

Investigation Procedures
The policy should describe how an investigation will be carried out, ensuring confidentiality and impartiality.

Disciplinary Actions
Clear possible outcomes for confirmed cases of harassment should be outlined, ranging from warnings and mandatory training to termination.

Protection Against Retaliation
The policy should explicitly state that no employee will face retaliation for reporting harassment.

Implementation and Communication

Employee Training
Regular training sessions should be conducted to educate employees about harassment and the policy.

Management Training
Specific training for managers and HR personnel should be provided to handle complaints effectively.

Availability
The policy should be easily accessible to all employees, whether in the employee handbook, company intranet, or posted in communal spaces.

Regular Updates
The policy should be reviewed and updated regularly to align with any changes in laws or organizational structures.

Case Studies

Company A - A lack of clear harassment policy led to a lawsuit that not only cost money but damaged the company's reputation.

Company B - With a strong harassment policy and training programs, Company B successfully created a respectful work environment, mitigating legal risks and improving employee satisfaction.

Harassment policies serve as both a preventive and corrective measure against workplace hostility. An effective policy not only sets the behavioral norms but also provides a framework for reporting and investigating complaints, thus safeguarding both the employees and the organization. In the next chapter, we will delve into practical steps and proactive measures that can be taken to build a work environment that is not just free from hostility, but encourages mutual respect and collaboration.

Reporting Mechanisms - The Cornerstone of Accountability

Reporting mechanisms are critical in enabling a culture of accountability within an organization. Without an effective, trustworthy process for employees to report harassment or discrimination, even the best harassment policies will remain mere paperwork. This section delves into what constitutes effective reporting mechanisms, how they should be implemented, and why they are a cornerstone in dealing with hostile work environments.

Importance of Robust Reporting Mechanisms

Provides an Outlet for Targets and Bystanders:
A functional reporting system enables those affected by harassment, as well as witnesses, to come forward without fear of retribution.

Facilitates Timely Intervention:
Prompt reporting allows for immediate action, potentially halting damaging behavior before it escalates further.

Fosters Trust in the Organization:
A transparent and effective reporting mechanism can

bolster trust in the organization, making employees feel heard and protected.

Essential Features of Reporting Mechanisms

Multiple Avenues for Reporting
Having more than one avenue for reporting ensures that individuals can bypass their immediate supervisors in case they are the harassers or enablers.

Confidentiality
Reporting should be as confidential as possible to protect the identity and integrity of the complainant.

Third-Party Involvement
Some organizations use third-party ombudsmen or hotlines to ensure impartiality.

Easy Accessibility
The reporting mechanism should be easily accessible and user-friendly to encourage use.

Documentation
Clear guidelines should be available for documenting incidents effectively, which can serve as vital evidence later on.

Common Reporting Channels

Human Resources
HR typically serves as the primary channel for reporting harassment.

Management
Direct supervisors or managers can be another

channel, especially if they are trained to handle such complaints.

Online Platforms
Anonymous online reporting platforms are increasingly being used to collect complaints.

Hotlines
Toll-free numbers for anonymous reporting can also be an effective tool, especially when managed by a third-party.

Ombudsman
Some larger organizations employ an ombudsman to handle complaints impartially.

Overcoming Barriers to Reporting

Fear of Retaliation
The reporting mechanism should explicitly assure protection against retaliation and have systems in place to enforce it.

Lack of Awareness
Regular training and communication can help ensure that all employees are aware of how and where to report harassment.

Complexity
The process should be streamlined and easy to understand, removing unnecessary bureaucratic hurdles.

Accountability and Follow-Up

A reporting mechanism should not just collect complaints but also be part of a larger system that ensures timely investigation, appropriate action, and follow-up to assess the resolution's effectiveness.

Reporting mechanisms are not just procedural formalities; they are an integral part of an organization's defense against harassment and hostility. A well-designed and properly implemented reporting mechanism fosters a culture of trust and accountability, empowering employees to stand up against harassment and making the workplace safer for everyone.

Real-Life Historical Example: Civil Rights Act of 1964 (United States)

The Civil Rights Act of 1964 is a landmark piece of legislation in the United States that had a profound impact on combating discrimination, particularly racial discrimination, and shaping the legal framework for equal rights in the workplace. This example illustrates the historical development of legal frameworks and responsibilities related to workplace discrimination.

Legal Framework and Responsibilities:

Background: Before the Civil Rights Act of 1964, racial segregation and discrimination were pervasive in the United States, including in the workplace. African Americans faced systemic discrimination, with limited access to jobs, education, and equal treatment in public spaces.

Key Provisions: The Civil Rights Act of 1964 outlawed discrimination on the basis of race, color, religion, sex, or national origin in various settings, including employment. Key provisions related to the workplace included:

Title VII: Title VII of the Act prohibits discrimination in employment practices based on race, color, religion, sex, or national origin. It established the Equal Employment Opportunity Commission (EEOC) to enforce these provisions.

Responsibilities of Employers: The Act placed significant responsibilities on employers. They were required to:

- Ensure equal employment opportunities for all employees and job applicants.
- Refrain from discriminatory hiring, firing, or promotion practices.
- Address workplace harassment and create policies to prevent discrimination.

Enforcement: The EEOC was established to enforce Title VII. It investigates complaints of workplace discrimination, engages in legal action against employers who violate the law, and seeks remedies for victims of discrimination.

Impact:

The Civil Rights Act of 1964 had a transformative

impact on the United States:

- It marked a turning point in the struggle for civil rights and equality, contributing to the broader civil rights movement.

- It paved the way for increased workplace diversity and equal opportunities for people of all races and backgrounds.

- The Act has been used in numerous legal cases to challenge discriminatory practices, setting legal precedents and shaping the legal framework for equal employment rights.

This historical example illustrates how a legal framework, in this case, the Civil Rights Act of 1964, can establish clear responsibilities for employers and enforce equal rights in the workplace. It serves as a powerful example of how legislation can lead to significant societal change by addressing historical inequalities and promoting equal opportunities.

PART II: SELF-CARE AND COPING STRATEGIES

CHAPTER 4

*Emotional and Mental
Well-being*

While we often focus on external factors like reporting mechanisms, harassment policies, and organizational culture to tackle hostile work environments, we must not overlook the significance of emotional and mental well-being. This chapter aims to shed light on how nurturing your emotional and mental health can serve as the foundation for resilience, thereby allowing you to better navigate challenging workplaces.

The Importance of Emotional and Mental Well-being

Self-Empowerment
A strong emotional and mental state enables you to assert yourself more effectively, standing up against

harassment or toxic behaviors.

Decision-Making
Sound emotional and mental health leads to better judgment and decision-making skills, critical for thriving in any environment, especially hostile ones.

Interpersonal Relationships
Maintaining emotional balance can improve your relationships with coworkers, superiors, and subordinates, potentially mitigating some elements of workplace hostility.

Components of Emotional and Mental Well-being

Emotional Intelligence
The ability to understand and manage both your emotions and those of others can be pivotal in dealing with workplace stressors.

Self-Esteem
A healthy sense of self-worth makes you less susceptible to the adverse impacts of hostility.

Coping Mechanisms
Effective coping strategies can help you deal with stress, preventing it from escalating into anxiety or other mental health issues.

Strategies for Nurturing Emotional and Mental Well-being

Professional Help
Consulting a therapist or counselor can provide

personalized coping strategies.

Journaling
Writing down your thoughts and emotions can serve as a self-reflective tool and emotional outlet.

Boundaries
Clearly setting professional and personal boundaries can significantly reduce stress.

Hobbies and Interests
Engaging in activities that bring joy can be a powerful antidote to workplace stress.

Mindfulness and Meditation
These practices, as discussed in the previous chapter, are also beneficial for emotional and mental well-being.

Work-Life Balance

Maintaining a healthy work-life balance can be particularly effective for emotional and mental well-being. Tips for achieving this include:

Prioritizing Tasks: Focus on what genuinely needs your attention at work and at home.

Taking Time Off: Make use of vacation days to recharge emotionally and mentally.

Family and Social Life: Don't neglect your social relationships; they are often the pillars supporting your well-being.

The Role of Employers

Employers can contribute significantly by:

Promoting a Healthy Culture: A culture that values emotional and mental well-being will naturally reduce hostility.

Providing Resources: Employers can offer Employee Assistance Programs (EAPs), mental health days, and other resources.

Limitations

While personal well-being is vital, it is not a panacea. Structural issues within the organization must also be addressed for lasting change.

Emotional and mental well-being are often the unsung heroes in the fight against hostile work environments. By prioritizing your well-being, you not only safeguard your health but also equip yourself with the tools needed to thrive in challenging conditions.

Building Resilience
Your Personal Shield in a Hostile Environment

While systemic changes are crucial for eradicating hostile work environments, personal resilience plays an equally important role in navigating these challenging situations. Resilience empowers you to maintain your well-being and continue performing effectively, even when facing adversity. This section will explore strategies for building resilience as a personal shield against hostility and stress.

Why Resilience Matters

Emotional Equilibrium
Building resilience helps you maintain emotional stability, providing the mental fortitude to cope with negative situations.

Performance
Resilient individuals are often better at managing stress, which allows them to maintain or even improve performance under challenging conditions.

Well-being
Enhanced resilience can lead to better mental and physical health, reducing the risk of stress-related illnesses.

Components of Resilience

Self-Awareness
Understanding your triggers and stressors is the first step in developing resilience. This enables you to know people and situation to avoid and what to embrace.

Emotional Regulation
Being able to manage your emotions, especially in high-stress situations, is crucial. It is a great virtue to be able to stay calm and rational under stress.

Optimism
A positive outlook can change how you interpret and respond to stressful situations. This will help you address things properly without bias from preconceived negative notions.

Social Support
Maintaining a strong social network can provide emotional sustenance, which is vital for resilience. This could be your work colleagues, friends or family members.

Problem-Solving Skills
Effective problem-solving abilities allow you to identify solutions rather than getting overwhelmed by challenges.

Strategies for Building Resilience

Self-Care
Prioritize activities that rejuvenate you, be it exercise, hobbies, or spending time with loved ones.

Mindfulness and Meditation
These practices have been shown to improve mental well-being and resilience.

Cognitive Reframing
Learn to reframe negative thoughts and perspectives into more positive and constructive ones.

Skill Building
Developing new skills can enhance your self-efficacy, increasing your resilience.

Seeking Professional Help
Therapists, counselors, or coaches can provide tailored strategies for building resilience.

Implementing Resilience in the Workplace

Cultivate a Supportive Network
Connect with supportive colleagues or mentors within the workplace.

Set Boundaries
Clearly delineate your work-life balance and maintain it.

Engage in Continuous Learning
Always look for opportunities for personal and professional growth, as this builds resilience over time.

Take Breaks and Time Off
Allow yourself to rest and recuperate to better deal with workplace stress.

Challenges and Limitations
While resilience is a powerful tool, it is not a substitute for systemic changes needed to remedy a hostile work environment. Personal resilience should complement, not replace, organizational solutions.

Resilience is your personal armor in navigating a hostile work environment. By investing in building your resilience, you equip yourself with the tools needed to cope with adversity while maintaining your performance and well-being.

Mindfulness and Stress Management - Tools for Inner Calm

In a hostile work environment, stress can escalate quickly, affecting not just your work performance but also your mental and physical health. This chapter aims to provide you with practical tools like mindfulness and stress management techniques that can be your sanctuary amid workplace turbulence.

The Connection Between Mindfulness and Stress Reduction

Mindfulness
Mindfulness is the practice of paying full attention to the present moment without judgment. By engaging in mindfulness, you cultivate a non-reactive approach to stressors.

Stress Reduction
Stress is often exacerbated by our thoughts and reactions to a situation. Mindfulness helps you observe these stressors without immediately reacting, providing room for more thoughtful responses.

Techniques for Practicing Mindfulness

Breath Awareness
Focusing on your breath can anchor your attention in the present moment. This is a straightforward method that can be practiced anywhere.

Body Scan
Involves mentally scanning your body from head to toe, noting sensations, and releasing tension.

Mindful Eating
Taking the time to fully experience the act of eating can turn a mundane activity into a practice of mindfulness.

Guided Meditation
Apps or recorded guided sessions can help you engage in mindfulness if you find it challenging to do it alone.

Stress Management Strategies

Time Management
Being in control of your time can significantly reduce stress levels. Use tools like to-do lists, calendars, and priority setting to manage your time effectively.

Exercise
Physical activity releases endorphins, which naturally alleviate stress.

Social Support
Maintaining a strong social network provides emotional support and an avenue for stress release.

Professional Help
Therapists and counselors can provide coping strategies tailored specifically for you.

Benefits of Mindfulness and Stress Management in the Workplace

Improved Focus
Mindfulness enhances your ability to concentrate, making you more productive.

Emotional Regulation
Being mindful can make it easier to control emotional responses to workplace stressors, reducing conflict and improving relationships.

Enhanced Creativity
A calm and focused mind is often more adept at creative problem-solving.

Better Health
Both mindfulness and stress management can lead to improved mental and physical health, including lower blood pressure, better sleep, and reduced anxiety.

Incorporating Mindfulness and Stress Management into Daily Routine

Micro-Breaks
Taking short breaks to practice mindfulness or stress-relief techniques can rejuvenate your mind.

Daily Rituals
Incorporate these practices into daily rituals, like during your commute or a specific time of the day set aside for self-care.

Mindfulness Reminders
Set reminders on your phone or computer to take mindful moments.

Limitations and Considerations

While mindfulness and stress management are potent tools, they are part of a broader strategy for dealing with a hostile work environment. They should not be seen as a complete solution but rather as complementary to other approaches.

Mindfulness and stress management can be your personal sanctuaries in a hostile work environment. These tools, when used consistently and effectively, can significantly enhance your resilience and overall well-being.

Real-Life Case: Whistleblower at Wells Fargo (2016)

The Wells Fargo whistleblower case is a poignant real-life example that highlights the emotional and mental well-being problems that can arise in a hostile work environment, especially when unethical practices are involved.

Background:

Wells Fargo, one of the largest banks in the United States, faced a massive scandal in 2016. The bank's employees were discovered to have engaged in fraudulent activities, including opening unauthorized customer accounts to meet aggressive sales targets. The intense pressure to achieve these targets and the hostile work environment it created played a significant role in the unfolding crisis.

Key Elements and Impact:

Pressure and Sales Targets: Employees at Wells Fargo were subjected to relentless sales targets and pressure to cross-sell products to customers. Failure to meet these targets resulted in disciplinary actions, including job loss.

Hostile Work Environment: The hostile work environment was characterized by unrealistic quotas, constant surveillance, and fear of retaliation for not meeting sales goals. Employees reported feeling immense stress and anxiety as they struggled to meet these targets.

Whistleblower's Experience: One Wells Fargo employee, a banker named Wells, became a whistleblower by reporting the fraudulent practices to higher-ups and regulatory authorities. Wells faced intense hostility and retaliation from coworkers and supervisors. She was ostracized and labeled a troublemaker, which took a toll on her emotional and mental well-being.

Impact and Results:

Wells Fargo's unethical practices, along with the hostile work environment created by the aggressive sales targets, led to severe emotional and mental well-being issues for many employees. Anxiety, stress, depression, and fear were common experiences.

The whistleblower, Wells, faced significant emotional distress due to the hostile reactions of her colleagues and supervisors. She became the subject of public scrutiny and faced retaliation within the organization.

The scandal resulted in legal action, regulatory fines, and damage to Wells Fargo's reputation. The bank was required to compensate affected customers and make significant changes to its corporate culture and practices.

This real-life case underscores the emotional and mental well-being problems that can arise in a hostile work environment driven by unethical practices and extreme performance pressure. It also highlights the importance of whistleblowers who, despite facing adversity, play a critical role in exposing wrongdoing and ultimately bringing about positive change in workplace environments.

CHAPTER 5

Documenting the Unthinkable

When it comes to navigating a hostile work environment, the importance of record-keeping cannot be overstated. Proper documentation serves as a robust form of evidence, should you decide to report harassment, discrimination, or any other form of misconduct. This chapter will walk you through why you need to maintain records, what to document, and how to do it effectively.

Why Record-keeping is Critical

Evidentiary Support
Documents can provide objective, factual evidence that supports your case when you report harassment or other issues.

Memory Fidelity
Our memories are not perfect; keeping records

ensures that you don't forget important details over time.

Empowerment
Having a detailed account of incidents gives you a sense of control and can empower you to take appropriate actions.

Accountability
Records make it easier to hold the responsible parties accountable, both legally and within the organization.

What to Document

Incidents and Interactions
Note down any adverse incidents or interactions, complete with dates, times, locations, and people involved.

Witnesses
Include names and contact information of any witnesses, if applicable.

Actions Taken
Document any steps you've taken, such as reporting the incident to your superiors or Human Resources.

Correspondence
Maintain records of all relevant emails, text messages, and other communications related to the issue.

Policy Information
Reference any company policies or guidelines that are related to your case.

Methods for Effective Record-keeping

Digital Documents
Create digital files, preferably with password protection, where you store scanned copies or digital notes of incidents.

Physical Files
For those who prefer analog methods, maintain a physical file where you keep printed emails, handwritten notes, and other relevant material.

Audio/Visual Records
While controversial and sometimes legally complicated, audio or visual recordings can sometimes serve as compelling evidence. Be sure you understand the legal ramifications in your jurisdiction before going this route.

Time-stamping
Ensure that all records are dated and, if possible, time-stamped for accuracy.

Confidentiality
Make sure your records are stored in a secure, confidential location, be it digital or physical.

Legal Considerations
Before you start keeping records, familiarize yourself with privacy laws and regulations relevant to your jurisdiction. While documentation is vital, it must be done in a legally compliant manner.

Using Records for Reporting and Legal Proceedings

If you decide to report the issue or take legal action, your records can serve as a vital part of your evidence, making it easier for investigative bodies to understand and assess your situation.

Record-keeping is a critical, often overlooked aspect of navigating a hostile work environment. By maintaining detailed, organized records, you equip yourself and authorities with the tools necessary for holding wrongdoers accountable. Proper documentation can make the difference between a case that is easily dismissed and one that leads to meaningful action. In the next chapter, we will delve into how collective action can serve as a powerful catalyst for changing hostile work environments.

What, When, and How to Document - The Fine Art of Keeping Records

If you've ever felt overwhelmed by the idea of documenting incidents in a hostile work environment, you're not alone. Knowing what to capture, when to capture it, and how to securely store this information can be confusing. This chapter aims to remove the guesswork from the equation by providing a straightforward guide to effective documentation.

What to Document

Specific Incidents

- Harassment, intimidation, or any form of discrimination.
- Unfair treatment or problematic interactions.
- Discrepancies between your work assessments and actual performance, if they contribute to a hostile environment.

Conversations

- Details of conversations that include threats, insinuations, or problematic comments.

Company Policies

- If policies regarding harassment or workplace behavior are not followed, this is worth documenting.

Retaliation

- Document any instances where you or others face retaliation for reporting incidents or standing up against hostility.

Supporting Materials

- Emails, text messages, or any other form of communication that corroborates your account.

When to Document

As Soon As Possible

- The best time to document an incident is immediately after it happens, when memories are fresh.

Regularly

- Consistency is key. Make it a routine to check and update your records periodically.

After Reporting

- Keep records of when you reported an issue and what actions were taken as a result.

How to Document

Digital Methods

✓ Use a secure app or document that is password-protected to ensure privacy.
✓ Time-stamp your entries for additional credibility.

Physical Methods

✓ Maintain a physical notebook dedicated solely to workplace incidents.
✓ Use ink (not pencil) for permanence and date each entry clearly.

Voice Recordings

✓ Some people find it quicker to speak rather than write. Voice recordings can be useful, but be cautious of consent laws in your jurisdiction.

Screenshots and Scans

✓ Capture digital evidence like emails or text

messages through screenshots or by scanning physical documents.

Third-Party Tools

✓   Some apps and platforms are designed for secure and anonymous reporting and documenting of workplace incidents.

Legal and Ethical Considerations

✓   Consult with a legal advisor to understand the boundaries of what you can document, especially if you are considering using audio or video recordings.

Storing Documentation

Secure Digital Storage

✓   Store your digital records in a secure cloud service that requires multi-factor authentication.

Safe Physical Storage

✓   Keep your physical records in a locked drawer or safe, away from the workplace if possible.

Knowing what, when, and how to document can be your most significant asset in dealing with a hostile work environment. Documentation lends weight to your experience, offering a more substantial basis for any future investigations or legal actions.

Real-Life Case: The Enron Scandal (2001)

The Enron scandal is a well-documented real-life example that underscores the importance and use of documenting unethical behavior in a hostile work environment. This case not only exposed corporate wrongdoing but also highlighted the critical role of documentation in bringing about accountability.

Background:

Enron Corporation was once considered one of the most innovative and successful energy companies in the United States. However, in 2001, it became synonymous with corporate fraud and unethical practices that led to its dramatic downfall.

Key Elements and Importance of Documentation:

Unethical Practices: Inside Enron, a hostile work environment had developed due to unethical practices, including accounting fraud, financial manipulation, and deceptive reporting. Employees were under tremendous pressure to meet unrealistic financial targets.

Whistleblower: Sherron Watkins, an employee at Enron, played a pivotal role in exposing the company's fraudulent activities. She became a whistleblower by documenting her concerns about accounting irregularities and sending a detailed memo to Enron's then-CEO, Kenneth Lay.

The Watkins Memo: Watkins' memo, often referred to as the "Watkins Memo," meticulously documented her observations and concerns about Enron's financial practices. In it, she described the hostile work environment where employees were pressured to engage in unethical behavior.

External Investigations: The documentation provided by Sherron Watkins became a critical piece of evidence when external investigations were initiated into Enron's financial wrongdoing. This documentation helped investigators understand the extent of the unethical practices and the toxic culture within the company.

Impact and Results:

The Enron scandal led to the largest bankruptcy in U.S. history at the time, resulting in massive financial losses for investors and employees.

Sherron Watkins' documentation played a crucial role in exposing the fraudulent activities, leading to legal action against Enron executives and ultimately holding them accountable for their actions.

The scandal also prompted regulatory changes, including the Sarbanes-Oxley Act of 2002, which imposed stricter corporate governance and accounting regulations to prevent similar corporate fraud in the future.

This real-life case illustrates the importance of documenting unethical behavior in a hostile work environment. Sherron Watkins' detailed documentation not only exposed corporate wrongdoing but also helped bring about accountability and legal action. It serves as a powerful example of how documentation can be a catalyst for change and justice, even in the most challenging and hostile work environments.

CHAPTER 6

Creating a Support Network

I n the battle against hostile work environments, you are not an island. Navigating the emotional and psychological hurdles of such a setting can be isolating, draining, and profoundly challenging. Therefore, building a robust support network becomes not just beneficial but essential for survival and growth. This network can offer emotional sustenance, practical advice, and sometimes even legal guidance when things get complicated. In this chapter, we will delve into why a support network is indispensable, who should be in your network, and how to go about creating and maintaining these vital relationships. After all, even the most resilient individuals can benefit from a supportive community —be it within the workplace, in personal life, or professional circles outside the organization.

Finding Allies within the Organization

The Value of Internal Allies

Navigating a hostile work environment is a difficult endeavor, but you don't have to do it alone. Internal allies within your organization can offer a wealth of benefits, from emotional support to tangible help in reporting and resolving issues. An ally is not merely a friend but someone who actively supports you, is aware of the issues you're facing, and is willing to take steps—be they big or small—to help mitigate those challenges.

Identifying Potential Allies

Observe Behavior
Watch how people in the organization treat others, especially when they think no one is watching. Those who consistently show respect and integrity are good candidates.

Test the Waters
Engage in casual conversations with potential allies, gradually sharing more sensitive information to gauge their responses and willingness to support.

Look for Previous Advocacy
Employees who have shown a willingness to stand up against unfair practices or who have supported others in the past are prime candidates for allies.

Approaching Potential Allies

Be Direct but Discreet

Open up about your experiences, but be cautious not to put the other person at risk or in an uncomfortable situation. A private setting is generally the best place for such discussions.

Assess Risk
Consider the level of trust and potential repercussions before you share sensitive information. Always respect the other person's comfort level and potential risk in becoming an ally.

Reciprocity
Allies should not feel used. Make it clear that the relationship is a two-way street, where both parties are willing to support each other.

Nurturing the Relationship

Frequent Check-ins
Maintain regular communication to discuss new developments, shared concerns, and strategies for tackling issues.

Discretion
The importance of maintaining confidentiality cannot be stressed enough. Both parties should be committed to safeguarding each other's privacy.

Collective Efforts
Once trust is established, you can consider teaming up for more extensive initiatives, such as reporting an issue or proposing a change in company policy.

The Limitations

While internal allies can be invaluable, remember that they too are part of the same hostile environment and may have their limitations or face risks. Always respect their boundaries and never pressure them into actions they are uncomfortable with.

Finding and maintaining relationships with allies within your organization can be a game-changer in how you navigate a hostile work environment. Internal allies can offer various types of support, from emotional to practical, that can significantly impact your well-being and success in challenging settings.

Outside Resources and Support Groups

While having allies within your organization is invaluable, there's an equally critical need for external support. This chapter will explore the role of outside resources and support groups in helping you navigate a hostile work environment. Having a broader network can offer you perspectives and coping strategies you may not find internally and provide a more confidential space for discussing sensitive issues.

Professional Organizations and Associations

Peer Support
Joining a professional organization related to your field can provide you with access to others who have faced or are currently facing similar challenges.

Workshops and Training

Many organizations offer workshops on conflict resolution, harassment prevention, and other pertinent topics.

Networking
Networking can provide you with alternative job opportunities if you decide that leaving your current workplace is the best option.

Online Support Groups and Forums

Anonymity
Online platforms allow you to seek advice and share your experiences without revealing your identity, offering an extra layer of security.

24/7 Access
You can seek support at any time, a significant advantage for those moments when you need immediate advice or emotional support.

Diverse Perspectives
Online groups often include members from diverse professional backgrounds and industries, providing a wide range of insights.

Therapists and Counselors

Emotional Support
Trained professionals can offer you tools for coping with stress, anxiety, and other emotional tolls.

Confidentiality
What you share in therapy stays in therapy, providing

a secure environment to discuss your experiences.

Objective Advice
A therapist can give you impartial advice that friends or family might not offer.

Legal Advisors

Understanding Rights
Legal professionals can help you understand your rights and the appropriate steps to take if you decide to take legal action.

Strategy
A legal advisor can help you formulate a strategy for handling disputes and formal complaints, potentially with a better outcome.

Friends and Family

Don't underestimate the power of a strong personal support network. Friends and family offer emotional sustenance that can help you persevere in a challenging work environment.

Outside resources and support groups play a critical role in helping you cope with a hostile work environment. From professional associations to therapists and legal advisors, expanding your support network beyond your immediate workplace can provide you with the tools, emotional support, and advice you need to thrive.

Real-Life Case: Support Network at Uber (2017)

The case of Susan Fowler, a former Uber employee, is a real-life example that highlights the importance of creating a support network in a hostile work environment. Her experiences and the subsequent actions she took underscore the significance of solidarity and support when facing workplace challenges.

Background:

Susan Fowler joined Uber in 2015 as a site reliability engineer. During her time at the company, she faced a hostile work environment marked by sexual harassment, discrimination, and a lack of accountability.

Creating a Support Network:

Blogging Her Experience: Susan Fowler took the courageous step of documenting her experiences in a personal blog post titled "Reflecting On One Very, Very Strange Year At Uber." In her blog, she detailed instances of harassment and discrimination she had faced, as well as her unsuccessful attempts to seek help from HR and management.

Sharing Her Story Publicly: Fowler's blog post went viral, sparking a wave of support and outrage from individuals within and outside the tech industry. Her willingness to share her story publicly resonated with many who had faced similar challenges in their own workplaces.

Building a Supportive Community: Fowler's actions led to the creation of a supportive community, both online and offline. Many individuals, including current and former Uber employees, reached out to offer support, share their own experiences, and advocate for change within the company.

Impact and Results:

Fowler's blog post and the ensuing public outcry had a profound impact. It triggered an internal investigation at Uber, which resulted in the termination of several employees and the implementation of various reforms and policy changes.

The case also had wider implications for the tech industry and workplace environments in general. It contributed to a broader conversation about workplace harassment, discrimination, and the importance of building support networks to address such issues.

Susan Fowler's actions were instrumental in bringing about change not only within Uber but also in inspiring others to speak out against hostile work environments and demand accountability.

This real-life case underscores the importance of creating a support network when facing a hostile work environment. Susan Fowler's decision to share her experiences and build a community of supporters played a crucial role in exposing wrongdoing, bringing about change, and empowering others to address similar challenges in their own workplaces.

PART III: NAVIGATING THE SYSTEM

CHAPTER 7

Reporting: When and How

One of the most crucial decisions you'll face when dealing with a hostile work environment is when to formally report the issues you're experiencing. This decision is often a complex one, fraught with emotional and practical considerations. While there's no one-size-fits-all answer, this chapter will guide you through the variables you should consider to make the most informed decision possible.

Severity of the Situation

Immediate Danger
If you are in a situation where your immediate safety or that of your colleagues is at risk, reporting as soon as possible is crucial.

Legal Violations
When the hostility involves breaking laws, such as

cases of sexual harassment or racial discrimination, prompt reporting is advisable.

Escalating Behavior
When the problematic behavior is showing signs of escalation, it might be time to report before things get worse.

Your Level of Preparedness

Documentation
Ensure that you have adequately documented instances of harassment, discrimination, or other forms of hostility.

Witnesses
Having credible witnesses can lend weight to your claims and make it easier for an investigation to substantiate your report.

Emotional Readiness
Reporting can be emotionally taxing. Assess your emotional state and ensure you're ready for the steps that come after reporting.

Company Policies and Procedures

Know the Process
Be aware of your company's procedures for reporting harassment or discrimination. This will give you an idea of what to expect after you report.

Statute of Limitations
Some organizations have reporting time limits after

an incident occurs. Make sure you're aware of these limitations, if any.

Potential Repercussions

Retaliation
Unfortunately, reporting can sometimes lead to retaliatory behavior. Weigh the benefits of reporting against the risks.

Professional Repercussions
Consider the possible impacts on your career, both within your current organization and in your broader professional life.

Outside Advice

Legal Counsel
Consulting a legal advisor can help you understand the implications of reporting and how to protect yourself.

Support Network
Discuss your situation with trusted members of your support network, both inside and outside the organization, to gain different perspectives.

Deciding when to report involves multiple considerations, including the severity of the situation, your level of preparedness, company policies, and potential repercussions. It's a decision that requires careful thought and, often, consultation with trusted advisors. While the timing will differ for everyone, understanding these factors can help you make a decision that aligns with your best interests.

Preparing Your Case - Laying the Groundwork for a Credible Complaint

Making the decision to report a hostile work environment is just the first step. The next, and equally crucial, step is preparing your case. A well-prepared case not only lends credibility to your complaint but also increases the chances of a thorough investigation and a favorable outcome. This section outlines the steps you need to take to build a solid case before officially reporting.

Gathering Documentation

Chronological Timeline
Create a detailed timeline of events, noting the dates, times, and locations of each incident. Also mention any witnesses present at the time.

Supporting Evidence
Compile any emails, text messages, voice recordings, or other types of communication that substantiate your claims.

Internal Records
If the company has previous records of complaints against the accused or concerning the hostile environment, these can strengthen your case.

Identifying Witnesses

Who to Approach

Look for witnesses who are willing to cooperate and whose accounts would lend credibility to your complaint.

Preparing Witnesses
Brief your witnesses on what to expect during an investigation and what kind of questions they might be asked.

Consult Outside Experts

Legal Advice
Prioritize consulting a legal advisor to understand the implications of your case and what protections you should seek.

Emotional Support
Therapists or counselors can provide emotional support, which can be vital when preparing a potentially draining legal case.

Understanding Company Policies

Employee Handbook
Review your organization's employee handbook or code of conduct to understand the policies regarding harassment and discrimination.

Reporting Mechanism
Understand the company's formal procedures for reporting and whom you should approach with your complaint.

Preparing Your Statement

Written Documentation
Your initial complaint should be in writing and as detailed as possible. Utilize your chronological timeline to structure your account.

Emotional Preparedness
Be mentally prepared to discuss uncomfortable or painful details, as you might have to recount them multiple times during an investigation.

Considering Confidentiality

Anonymity
Evaluate the pros and cons of anonymous reporting if your organization offers it. It can protect you from immediate retaliation but may limit the investigation's scope.

Safeguarding Witnesses
Consider how to best protect the identity of your witnesses, especially if they're still part of the organization.

Preparing your case is a meticulous process that demands attention to detail, a comprehensive gathering of evidence, and thorough mental preparation. Taking the time to lay this groundwork can make all the difference in how your complaint is received and acted upon. Your preparation will not only help the investigation but also sets the stage for what comes after—whether that's legal action, internal disciplinary measures, or organizational change. In the next chapter, we'll delve into what to expect once you've submitted your complaint and how to navigate the investigation process.

Following Through - Navigating the Post-Reporting Landscape

Submitting your complaint marks the beginning of a new phase in your journey through a hostile work environment. While the case is being investigated, it's important to know how to navigate the complexities and challenges you may face. This chapter will help you understand the steps you should take post-reporting, from following company procedures to managing emotional tolls.

Staying Informed

Regular Updates
Stay updated on the progress of the investigation. It's your right to know how your complaint is being handled.

Communication Channels
Identify and establish regular lines of communication with the person or team responsible for the investigation.

Emotional Preparedness

Support Network
Keep in touch with your internal and external support networks for emotional and psychological support.

Self-Care

Invest in self-care activities to manage the stress and emotional toll that may come with the reporting process.

Interacting with the Accused and Witnesses

Neutral Environment
Try to maintain a neutral environment if you still have to work closely with the accused or the witnesses.

No Retaliation
Be aware of your actions to ensure they can't be perceived as retaliatory, which could complicate your case.

Maintaining Documentation

New Incidents
Continue to document any new incidents related to the hostile environment, as they can be pertinent to the ongoing investigation.

Conversations
Keep a record of conversations that relate to your complaint or the investigation, as they may become crucial later on.

Legal Aspects

Employment Laws
Be aware of the employment laws related to your case and understand your rights under these laws.

Legal Representation

If things escalate or if the investigation isn't moving forward, you might need to consult legal professionals again for advice or representation.

Possible Outcomes

Organizational Action
This could range from training programs, to disciplinary actions against the accused, or even changes in management.

Legal Recourse
If the internal investigation is unsatisfactory, you may need to consider external legal options.

Moving Forward

Recovery and Resilience
Whether you decide to stay in the organization or move on, focus on your recovery and resilience to navigate future challenges.

Sharing Your Story
Consider sharing your experiences in appropriate forums to help others who may be in similar situations.

Following through after reporting is a phase of continued vigilance, emotional resilience, and possible legal complexities. By staying informed, maintaining ongoing documentation, and leaning on your support network, you can navigate this challenging time more effectively. This chapter should serve as a roadmap for what to expect and how to handle the myriad issues that can arise post-reporting.

Real-Life Case: The #MeToo Movement (2017 - Present)

The #MeToo movement is a powerful real-life example that demonstrates the importance of reporting incidents of harassment and misconduct in the context of a hostile work environment. This global movement has encouraged individuals to come forward with their experiences and demand accountability from those responsible.

Background:

The #MeToo movement gained momentum in October 2017 when allegations of sexual harassment and assault against Hollywood producer Harvey Weinstein were widely reported. This case highlighted not only the prevalence of sexual misconduct but also the barriers that individuals often face when reporting such incidents, especially in high-profile and male-dominated industries.

Reporting: When and How:

Initial Disclosures: Several women, including actresses like Ashley Judd and Rose McGowan, publicly shared their experiences of harassment and assault by Harvey Weinstein. Their courageous disclosures opened the floodgates for others to come forward.

Social Media: The #MeToo hashtag quickly spread across social media platforms, with individuals from all walks of life sharing their stories of harassment and assault. This online movement provided a safe space for survivors to report their experiences and support one another.

Traditional Reporting: While many stories were initially shared on social media, they often led to formal reports and legal actions. Many survivors reported their experiences to law enforcement, human resources departments, and legal authorities, initiating investigations and legal proceedings.

Impact and Results: The #MeToo movement has had a profound impact on raising awareness of sexual harassment and assault in workplaces, schools, and communities worldwide. It has led to the exposure and accountability of high-profile individuals, changes in corporate policies, and legal reforms.

Key Takeaways:

The #MeToo movement illustrates the power of collective reporting. When individuals shared their stories, they not only found support but also exposed systemic issues and patterns of misconduct.

Social media played a significant role in amplifying survivors' voices and breaking down the barriers to reporting. It provided a platform for individuals to disclose their experiences and demand justice.

The movement highlighted the importance of addressing hostile work environments and the need for organizations to have clear reporting mechanisms, support systems, and a commitment to taking action against harassers.

This real-life example demonstrates that reporting incidents of harassment and misconduct in a hostile work environment can have far-reaching consequences. By coming forward and sharing their experiences, survivors within the #MeToo movement not only brought perpetrators to justice but also initiated broader conversations about the importance of reporting and creating safer workplaces for all.

CHAPTER 8

Conversations with HR and Management

Engaging with Human Resources (HR) and management is an inevitable part of reporting and resolving issues related to a hostile work environment. These conversations can often feel intimidating, laden with corporate jargon and an undertone of scrutiny. However, they're also an opportunity to make your case, influence change, and seek justice or resolution.

This chapter aims to prepare you for these crucial interactions, offering guidance on how to approach them, what to expect, and how to protect your interests. Whether you're talking to an HR representative, your direct manager, or even higher-level executives, understanding the nuances and expectations of these conversations can significantly impact the outcome of your complaint and future well-being in the organization.

What to Expect - The Unspoken Realities of HR and Management Conversations

When you decide to report hostile work behavior to HR or management, your expectations may range from hopeful to skeptical. While HR departments are designed to resolve internal conflicts and protect employee welfare, they also have the company's interests in mind. Similarly, management may want to solve the problem but could be constrained by corporate culture or other variables. Here's what you can generally expect when navigating these conversations:

Initial Contact

Formality
Expect a formal atmosphere during your initial conversation, which may involve paperwork and procedural steps to officially register your complaint.

Neutral Tone
HR representatives are trained to maintain a neutral tone. Don't be discouraged if they don't immediately validate your experiences; it's their job to gather facts impartially.

Questioning and Fact-Finding

Detailed Queries
Be prepared to answer detailed questions about your

experience, as HR will want to get a thorough understanding of the situation.

Documentation Request
You may be asked to submit any evidence or documentation you've gathered, such as emails, text messages, or a written account of incidents.

Timelines

Investigation Period
HR will often provide you with a timeline for the investigation. This can vary widely depending on the severity and complexity of the case.

Follow-Ups
Expect periodic follow-ups either to gather additional information or to update you on the investigation's progress.

Emotional Dynamics

Stress and Anxiety
It's natural to feel anxious or stressed before, during, and after these conversations. Prepare yourself mentally and emotionally.

Emotional Detachment
While you may be emotionally invested in the situation, HR and management are likely to approach it from a procedural standpoint. It's crucial not to mistake this detachment for apathy.

Possible Outcomes

Varied Reactions
Management and HR may react differently to your complaint, depending on the severity, the people involved, and how the situation impacts the organization.

Potential for Change
These conversations can lead to a variety of outcomes, from policy changes and staff retraining to disciplinary actions against offenders.

Legal Implications

Confidentiality
Though these conversations are often confidential, be aware that HR may have to disclose details as part of a legal requirement or internal process.

Legal Rights
It may also be advisable to consult a legal advisor before or after speaking with HR and management to ensure you fully understand your rights and the potential legal pathways available to you.

By understanding what to expect, you can go into these critical conversations with more confidence and preparedness, making it more likely that you will be able to advocate effectively for yourself.

Possible Outcomes - The Aftermath of Reporting to HR and Management

Once you've had your conversations with HR and management, several possible outcomes may emerge, ranging from internal resolutions to legal implications. It's essential to understand what these potential pathways are so you can prepare for them and make informed decisions about your next steps. This section delves into what you might expect after reporting a hostile work environment.

Internal Company Actions

Verbal or Written Warnings to the Offender
The most immediate step a company may take is to issue warnings to the person or persons responsible for creating the hostile work environment.

Sensitivity Training
Organizations often conduct mandatory sensitivity or anti-harassment training following a complaint.

Job Reassignment
In some cases, either you or the accused may be reassigned to different departments or projects to minimize interaction.

Promotions, Demotions, and Terminations
Depending on the severity of the case and the findings of the investigation, job roles may be altered, or the offender may be terminated.

Legal Consequences

Internal Investigations

HR may conclude their internal investigation, which could lead to company-sanctioned penalties against the perpetrator, such as fines or even legal action.

External Investigations
In more severe cases or if the internal investigation is unsatisfactory, you might opt for legal proceedings, involving external bodies like employment tribunals or civil courts.

Settlements
Sometimes, the case may be resolved through a negotiated settlement, which could include financial compensation, nondisclosure agreements, or other terms.

Emotional and Psychological Impact

Vindication or Frustration
The outcome of your report can result in a range of emotional responses, from relief and vindication to frustration and disillusionment.

Workplace Atmosphere
Depending on how the situation is handled, there could be a noticeable change in workplace atmosphere — either more positive due to resolution or tense due to unresolved issues.

Impact on Career

Reputation
Your reputation within the company could be affected, either positively as someone who stood up

for the right thing or negatively if the issue isn't resolved satisfactorily.

Professional Development
Outcomes can also have long-term implications for your career growth and professional development.

Long-term Organizational Change

Policy Adjustments
Your actions might lead to long-lasting changes in company policy related to harassment and discrimination.

Cultural Shift
In the best-case scenario, resolving the issue effectively can contribute to a more inclusive and respectful workplace culture.

The outcomes of reporting a hostile work environment to HR and management are varied and can be influenced by multiple factors, such as the severity of the offense, company culture, and the effectiveness of the internal investigation. While some results may offer immediate relief, others may require long-term adjustments, both personally and professionally. Understanding these possible outcomes can help you manage your expectations and prepare for future steps, whether within your current organization or in new career paths.

Handling Retaliation - Protecting Yourself in the Aftermath

Reporting a hostile work environment is a courageous act, but it can sometimes result in retaliation from the accused party, their allies, or even the organization itself. Understanding how to identify and cope with retaliatory actions is crucial for protecting your interests and well-being. This section offers guidance on what retaliation might look like, how to document it, and what actions you can take to safeguard yourself.

Identifying Retaliation

Subtle Changes
Sometimes retaliation isn't overt; it manifests as subtle shifts in behavior such as exclusion from meetings, lack of communication, or sudden unsatisfactory performance reviews.

Open Hostility
In more blatant cases, you may face direct confrontations, public humiliation, or increased harassment.

Professional Setbacks
Retaliation may also appear as demotion, reduced responsibilities, or being passed over for promotions or opportunities.

Legal Context

Federal and State Laws
Retaliation   for   reporting   harassment   or

discrimination is illegal under federal laws like Title VII of the Civil Rights Act of 1964, and often under state laws as well.

Legal Protection
Understanding the scope of legal protections against retaliation can empower you to take action.

Documentation and Evidence

Continuous Record-Keeping
Just like you documented the initial hostile behavior, continue to document instances of retaliation meticulously.

Witness Accounts
Corroborating your experience with witness accounts can strengthen your case against retaliation.

Responding to Retaliation

Internal Reporting
Report retaliatory actions to HR and management, following the procedures you used for the initial complaint.

Legal Recourse
Consult a legal advisor to explore your options, which may include filing a retaliation claim or even initiating a lawsuit.

Building Resilience

Emotional Support
Reconnect with your support network, both within

and outside of the organization, to help you navigate through retaliation.

Self-Care Strategies
Focusing on mental well-being through techniques like mindfulness or stress management can help you remain resilient during this challenging period.

Long-Term Strategies

Assessing the Work Environment
Sometimes, the best course of action might be to evaluate whether the current organization aligns with your long-term career and emotional well-being.

Professional Alternatives
Prepare yourself for possible career changes such as job transition or even industry shift, so you're not cornered into tolerating retaliatory behavior.

Retaliation is an unfortunate but real risk when reporting a hostile work environment. However, being prepared can mitigate risks and offer you routes for action and resolution. In understanding the forms retaliation can take, and the steps you can follow to address it, you are better positioned to protect your career and personal well-being.

Real-Life Case: Uber's Cultural Transformation (2017)

The case of Uber's cultural transformation in 2017 is a real-life example of conversations with HR and management in the context of a hostile work environment. This case illustrates how addressing a hostile workplace culture requires direct dialogue, significant changes, and the involvement of top management.

Background:

Uber, a ride-sharing technology company, faced a series of scandals and controversies in 2017, including allegations of sexual harassment, discrimination, and a toxic work culture. The company's reputation was tarnished, and its employees, particularly women and minority groups, faced a hostile work environment.

Conversations with HR and Management:

Susan Fowler's Revelations: Susan Fowler, a former Uber engineer, wrote a detailed blog post in February 2017, describing her experiences of sexual harassment, discrimination, and the company's failure to address her complaints. Her blog post initiated a public conversation about the workplace culture at Uber.

Internal Investigations: Uber initiated internal investigations into the allegations, led by former U.S. Attorney General Eric Holder and his law firm, Covington & Burling. These investigations involved conversations with current and former employees to gather information about the hostile work environment.

CEO's Involvement: Uber's CEO at the time, Travis Kalanick, was directly involved in addressing the issues. He held meetings with employees to listen to their concerns and participated in implementing changes to the company's policies and culture.

Conversations with HR: Uber's HR department played a crucial role in addressing the hostile work environment. They conducted surveys and interviews with employees to assess the extent of the problems and gather input on potential solutions.

Impact and Results:

Uber's cultural transformation efforts included the firing of employees involved in misconduct, revising company policies, implementing mandatory diversity and inclusion training, and appointing a new Chief Diversity and Inclusion Officer.

Travis Kalanick stepped down as CEO, and the company underwent significant leadership changes, signaling a commitment to a cultural shift.

Uber's response to the crisis demonstrated the importance of addressing a hostile work environment through open conversations with HR and management, as well as the necessity of involving top leadership to drive change.

While challenges remained, the steps taken by Uber were seen as a significant effort to rebuild trust and create a more inclusive and respectful workplace environment.

This real-life example showcases the role of conversations with HR and management in addressing a hostile work environment. Uber's willingness to engage in difficult conversations, conduct internal investigations, and implement changes demonstrated a commitment to transforming its workplace culture and addressing the concerns of its employees.

CHAPTER 9

Considering Legal Action

W hen All Else Fails, Know Your Options. Despite best efforts to resolve issues internally, there may come a time when considering legal action becomes not just an option, but perhaps a necessity. Legal recourse can seem like a daunting path, fraught with complexities, uncertainties, and the emotional toll of litigation. Nevertheless, it serves as a crucial avenue for achieving justice and holding parties accountable for creating or perpetuating a hostile work environment.

This chapter aims to equip you with the foundational knowledge you'll need to navigate the legal landscape. We will discuss when it might be appropriate to consider taking legal action, what types of legal remedies might be available to you, and how to prepare for the legal process. Whether you're at the point of seeking external intervention or just want to understand all the cards in your hand, this chapter will offer insight into the legal pathway as a means to redress and resolution.

When to Consult an Attorney

Consulting an attorney can be a pivotal step in dealing with a hostile work environment. While it might seem like a last resort, sometimes it's beneficial to consult legal advice earlier rather than later. But when is the right time? This chapter aims to help you identify the ideal moments for reaching out to an attorney so that you can make the most informed decisions in your struggle for justice and fair treatment.

Early Indicators

Persistent Unresolved Issues
If you've attempted internal resolutions—speaking with HR, participating in mediation, filing complaints —but the hostile behavior continues, it may be time to consult an attorney.

Lack of Action from Management or HR
When your concerns are met with indifference, delays, or outright dismissal from the company, seeking legal advice can guide your next steps.

After Retaliation

Identifying Acts of Retaliation
If you experience any form of retaliation after reporting the hostility, such as demotion, exclusion,

or additional harassment, this is a strong indicator that you should consult an attorney immediately.

Legal Deadlines

Statutory Limitations
Employment laws often have time limitations for filing complaints. An attorney can provide information on these deadlines, ensuring you don't miss your window for legal action.

Complexity of the Case

Multiple Parties Involved
If the hostility involves multiple people, whether as perpetrators or victims, the complexity increases, making legal advice all the more crucial.

Unclear Company Policies
Ambiguous or poorly-worded company policies on harassment can make internal resolution difficult. An attorney can help interpret these guidelines in a legal context.

Financial and Emotional Costs

Cost-Benefit Analysis
Attorneys can help you conduct a realistic assessment of your situation, weighing the emotional and financial costs of pursuing legal action.

Preparing for Possible Termination

Protective Measures
If you suspect that you may be terminated as an act

of retaliation or as a means to "resolve" the issue, consulting an attorney can offer you ways to protect your interests.

Confidential Consultation

Initial Consultation
Many attorneys offer initial consultations for free or a nominal fee. This initial meeting can provide valuable insights into your case without requiring a significant commitment.

Consulting an attorney isn't a sign of defeat but a proactive measure to safeguard your rights. Understanding the best time to seek legal advice can greatly influence the outcome of your case. Whether you're facing a complex situation with multiple variables or you're simply not getting the resolution you need within your organization, timely legal counsel can prove to be invaluable.

Legal Procedures and Expectations

The decision to take legal action is often accompanied by a plethora of questions about what exactly the process entails, what are your responsibilities, and what outcomes you can reasonably expect. This section aims to demystify the legal procedures associated with combating a hostile work environment and sets the stage for what you can anticipate throughout this journey.

Filing an Initial Complaint

Federal and State Agencies
In the U.S., before you can bring a lawsuit for harassment or discrimination, you typically need to file a complaint with a relevant federal or state agency, such as the Equal Employment Opportunity Commission (EEOC).

Time Constraints
Remember that you have a limited window to file this complaint, usually within 180 or 300 days of the last discriminatory act, depending on the jurisdiction.

Required Documentation
Gather all relevant records, emails, text messages, and any other pieces of evidence to submit along with your complaint.

Investigation Phase

Company's Role
Even if you proceed with legal action, your company will likely conduct its internal investigation parallelly.

Cooperation
You may need to participate in interviews or provide additional evidence. Always consult your attorney before engaging in these activities.

Legal Discovery

Depositions and Interrogatories
Both parties will exchange information through legal mechanisms like depositions and interrogatories.

Document Requests
Your attorney will likely request official company records, emails, and other communications as part of the evidence-gathering process.

Settlement Discussions

Mediation
Before heading to court, both parties may agree to participate in mediation to resolve the issue amicably.

Settlement Offers
Be prepared to receive or make settlement offers at different stages of the process.

Going to Trial

Preparation
Your attorney will prepare you for court appearances, including how to provide testimony and handle cross-examinations.

Expected Duration
Legal proceedings can be lengthy and emotionally draining, sometimes taking years to resolve fully.

Possible Outcomes

Monetary Compensation
Financial restitution is a common outcome but not guaranteed.

Policy Changes
Your legal action could lead to policy changes within the organization.

Emotional and Psychological Impact
Win or lose, the process will likely have a lasting emotional impact.

Costs Involved

Legal Fees
The costs can be substantial, including attorney fees, court costs, and time away from work.

Contingency Fees
Some attorneys may work on a contingency basis, taking a percentage of any settlement or court-awarded damages.

Legal action is a complex, lengthy process that can offer a varying range of outcomes, both tangible and intangible. While it may offer closure and justice, it also comes with its own set of challenges and costs. Knowing what to expect can help you make informed decisions, prepare for the emotional and financial investments involved, and ultimately, pursue the justice and respect you deserve.

Costs vs. Benefits

Taking legal action against a hostile work environment is not a decision to be made lightly. While the potential for justice and systemic change is compelling, the emotional, temporal, and financial costs can be significant. This section will guide you through weighing the costs against the benefits of pursuing a legal course of action, enabling you to make an informed decision that aligns with your goals and circumstances.

The Costs

Financial Expenditure

Legal Fees
Hiring an attorney, court filings, gathering evidence, and other related activities can be costly.

Lost Wages
Court appearances and related legal activities might require time off work, potentially impacting your earnings.

Emotional and Psychological Toll

Stress and Anxiety
Legal proceedings can be emotionally draining and stressful.

Reputation Risk
Legal action could have potential repercussions on your professional reputation, even if you're in the right.

Time Investment

Lengthy Proceedings
Legal action can be a slow process, sometimes taking months or even years to resolve.

Work-Life Balance
The time commitment may also interfere with personal responsibilities and work commitments.

The Benefits

Monetary Compensation

Damages and Settlements
Successful legal action could result in significant financial compensation, covering both actual losses and emotional distress.

Systemic Change

Policy Updates
Your case may lead to policy changes that make the workplace safer for everyone.

Legal Precedent
In some instances, a successful lawsuit can set a legal precedent that protects others in similar situations.

Personal Validation

Closure
Winning a legal case can provide a sense of justice and closure that may not be achievable otherwise.

Self-Empowerment
Taking action can empower you to stand up for yourself and others, overcoming the sense of helplessness that often accompanies victimization.

Risk and Uncertainty

No Guaranteed Outcome
It's crucial to remember that legal action offers no guaranteed positive outcome and may result in

financial loss if unsuccessful.

Unpredictable Reactions
Your employer's reaction to your lawsuit is not entirely predictable and could range from constructive change to negative repercussions.

Making the Decision

Consult With Trusted Advisors
Engage in discussions with your attorney, financial advisors, and emotional support network to weigh the pros and cons tailored to your unique situation.

Conduct a Formal Analysis
Some individuals find it helpful to conduct a formal cost-benefit analysis, assigning potential value to both the costs and benefits to compare them objectively.

Deciding to take legal action is a complex decision that will significantly impact various facets of your life. Weighing the costs against the benefits will help you arrive at a reasoned choice, ensuring that you are fully aware of the stakes, risks, and potential rewards involved. While it is an intensely personal decision, being well-informed allows you to make that choice with clarity and confidence.

Real-Life Case: The Case of Gretchen Carlson vs. Roger Ailes and Fox News (2016)

The case of Gretchen Carlson, a former Fox

News anchor, is a prominent real-life example of considering legal action in the context of a hostile work environment. This case not only shed light on the issue of workplace harassment but also illustrates the process and outcomes of pursuing legal action.

Background:

Gretchen Carlson was a well-known television anchor and host at Fox News, one of the largest news networks in the United States. In July 2016, she filed a lawsuit against Roger Ailes, the then-CEO and Chairman of Fox News, alleging sexual harassment and a hostile work environment.

Considering Legal Action:

Allegations of Harassment: Gretchen Carlson's lawsuit detailed numerous instances of sexual harassment, inappropriate comments, and retaliation she experienced during her tenure at Fox News. She described a hostile work environment where harassment was pervasive.

Seeking Legal Counsel: After facing harassment and witnessing a culture of silence around the issue, Carlson decided to seek legal counsel and take action. She hired prominent attorney Nancy Erika Smith to represent her in the case.

Filing a Lawsuit: In her lawsuit, Carlson accused Roger Ailes of making unwanted sexual advances and engaging in retaliatory behavior when she rejected his advances. The lawsuit also alleged that Ailes had created a culture of harassment at Fox News.

Media Attention: The case garnered extensive media attention, leading to public awareness and discussions about workplace harassment and hostile work environments in high-profile organizations.

Impact and Results:

Roger Ailes resigned as Chairman and CEO of Fox News within weeks of the lawsuit being filed, and the network reached a settlement with Gretchen Carlson for $20 million, along with a public apology.

The case had a profound impact on the media industry and sparked a broader conversation about workplace harassment, the role of powerful figures in enabling such behavior, and the importance of reporting and pursuing legal action.

Following the lawsuit, several other women at Fox News came forward with allegations of harassment, leading to additional legal actions and changes within the organization's leadership and policies.

The #MeToo movement, which gained momentum in subsequent years, was in part inspired by cases like Gretchen Carlson's, highlighting the importance of reporting and pursuing legal remedies in cases of workplace harassment.

This real-life case illustrates how individuals can consider legal action in response to a hostile work environment, particularly in cases of harassment.

Gretchen Carlson's decision to pursue legal remedies not only held a powerful figure accountable but also contributed to a broader conversation about workplace harassment and the need for change in workplace cultures.

PART IV: PROACTIVE STRATEGIES

CHAPTER 10

Shaping Company Culture

Addressing a hostile work environment is not just about navigating immediate challenges or taking reactive measures; it's also about fostering a culture where such negativity doesn't take root in the first place. While individuals can report incidents and HR departments can enforce policies, truly impactful change comes from a holistic transformation of company culture.

The goal of this chapter is to shift the focus from merely surviving in a hostile environment to actively participating in shaping a culture that prioritizes respect, diversity, and inclusion. Here, we will explore the role each stakeholder plays—from top-level management to entry-level employees—in fostering a healthy work environment. This chapter will guide you through various strategies to influence the attitudes and behaviors within your organization, ensuring that the battle against workplace hostility extends beyond the legal courtroom or HR office and into the very ethos of the company.

Whether you're an employee, manager, or executive, the ideas and suggestions presented in this chapter will arm you with the tools and perspective needed to initiate meaningful change. After all, the ultimate victory over a hostile work environment is the creation of a culture where such hostility can no longer exist.

Influencing from Within

Grassroots Initiatives and the Power of the Individual

Change often starts with the actions of a single individual. While executive orders and company-wide policies are essential, there's an undeniable influence that comes from grassroots initiatives led by employees themselves. This section aims to empower you, whether you're an individual contributor or a middle manager, with actionable steps to effect change from within your organization.

Speak Up

Safe Channels
Utilize existing channels within your company where employees can safely express concerns and share insights.

Open Conversations

Encourage open dialogue about workplace culture, harassment, and discrimination issues in appropriate settings like team meetings or organized discussion forums.

Build Allies

Identify Sympathetic Parties
Not everyone will be on board with your initiative, but some will. Identify who these individuals are and engage them in your efforts.

Form an Employee Resource Group
Creating a formalized group around issues like diversity, equity, and inclusion can give you a louder collective voice.

Leverage Data

Conduct Surveys
Anonymous employee surveys can bring issues to light and provide statistical evidence to back your claims or ideas.

Monitor Metrics
Track metrics related to employee turnover, absenteeism, and productivity as they can serve as indicators of the culture within the organization.

Create Awareness

Training Programs
Volunteer to organize or contribute to training sessions aimed at educating employees about

the elements that contribute to a hostile work environment and how to avoid them.

Share Stories and Testimonials
Sometimes personal stories can be more impactful than numbers. Create platforms where people can share their experiences anonymously if they choose.

Seek Managerial Support

The Power of Influence
Managers often serve as the bridge between executive decisions and ground-level implementation. Their support can be crucial in getting initiatives off the ground.

Speak Their Language
Frame your arguments for change in a way that aligns with business goals, whether that be increased productivity, reduced turnover, or enhanced employee engagement.

Celebrate Small Wins

Acknowledge Progress
Creating a better company culture is a long game. Celebrate the small victories along the way to keep up momentum.

Build On Success
Use each success, no matter how small, as a stepping stone to bigger initiatives and broader change.

Influencing from within is about maximizing the

leverage you have as an individual to effect meaningful change. It's about taking the initiative and rallying others to your cause, and it's about creating a grassroots movement that can either complement or catalyze top-down initiatives. Never underestimate the power of the individual in shaping company culture; sometimes, the smallest stone creates the largest ripple.

Tools for Organizational Change

Transformational change in an organization doesn't happen in a vacuum or solely through wishful thinking. It requires the right tools, methods, and processes that can help translate good intentions into meaningful impact. This section aims to guide you through the available tools for effecting organizational change, focusing on how to employ them to create a workplace culture that's free from hostility and conducive to productivity and well-being.

Diagnostic Tools

Employee Engagement Surveys
Use standardized surveys to gauge the pulse of employee morale and identify potential problem areas.

SWOT Analysis
Conducting a Strengths, Weaknesses, Opportunities, and Threats (SWOT) analysis can reveal where your

organization stands concerning workplace culture.

Training Modules

Diversity and Inclusion Training
Dedicated programs to educate employees on diversity and inclusion are critical to shifting organizational paradigms.

Conflict Resolution Training
Equip employees with the tools to resolve interpersonal conflicts amicably and constructively.

Communication Platforms

Anonymous Reporting Systems
Invest in secure platforms where employees can report issues anonymously, thereby reducing the fear of retaliation.

Internal Social Networks
Utilize platforms that allow employees to share positive stories and recognize each other's contributions.

Policies and Handbooks

Code of Conduct
Regularly update the organizational code of conduct to include clear guidelines on acceptable behavior.

Anti-Harassment Policy
Ensure your anti-harassment policy is comprehensive, accessible, and effectively communicated to all employees.

Management Tools

360-Degree Feedback
Use 360-degree feedback systems that allow employees to provide confidential evaluations of their peers and supervisors.

Performance Metrics
Incorporate "soft" performance metrics related to teamwork and communication in addition to the conventional "hard" metrics like sales or output.

Accountability Mechanisms

HR Case Management Software
Utilize software that allows HR to track and manage reports of workplace harassment or discrimination effectively.

Compliance Audits
Regular audits by an external party can ensure that the organization is adhering to its stated policies and guidelines.

Employee Well-being Programs

EAP Services
Employee Assistance Programs (EAPs) can offer counseling and other services to employees dealing with workplace stress or harassment.

Wellness Initiatives
Programs focused on mental and physical health can contribute to general well-being, making it easier for

employees to tackle workplace challenges.

Creating a healthy work environment requires a multi-faceted approach involving a variety of tools and strategies. From diagnostic tools to identify problems to accountability mechanisms for enforcing policies, each tool has its role to play in the larger tapestry of organizational change. The key is to be systematic, inclusive, and intentional in their application, keeping in mind that the ultimate goal is to foster a culture of respect, inclusion, and collaboration.

Real-Life Case: IBM's Transformation Under Louis V. Gerstner Jr. (1993-2002)

The transformation of IBM under the leadership of Louis V. Gerstner Jr. serves as a real-life example of shaping company culture in a hostile work environment. During his tenure as CEO, Gerstner faced the challenge of revitalizing a struggling company plagued by internal turmoil and fostering a more positive and productive workplace culture.

Background:

In the early 1990s, IBM, once an industry leader in computing technology, faced significant challenges. The company was experiencing financial losses, stagnant innovation, and a hostile internal work environment marked by bureaucracy and inefficiency.

Shaping Company Culture:

Assessment of the Situation: Louis V. Gerstner Jr. took over as CEO of IBM in 1993. One of his first tasks was to assess the internal and external factors contributing to IBM's decline. He recognized the existence of a hostile work environment marked by internal rivalries, lack of teamwork, and resistance to change.

Cultural Transformation: Gerstner initiated a cultural transformation within the company. He emphasized the importance of collaboration, innovation, and customer-centricity. He challenged the existing corporate culture, which had become resistant to change and internally competitive.

Clear Communication: Gerstner communicated his vision for IBM's transformation clearly and consistently. He stressed the need for employees to work together toward common goals, highlighting the importance of a more positive and cooperative work environment.

Employee Development: IBM invested in employee development and training programs to enhance skills and adapt to the changing technology landscape. This investment was crucial in improving the overall workplace culture.

Results-Oriented: Gerstner shifted the company's focus from internal processes to customer satisfaction and results. This change in mindset helped employees see the value of their work and contributed to a more positive work environment.

Impact and Results:

IBM's cultural transformation, led by Louis V. Gerstner Jr., played a pivotal role in turning the company around. By fostering a more positive and collaborative work environment, IBM became more agile and responsive to market changes.

Under Gerstner's leadership, IBM's financial performance improved significantly, and the company regained its status as a leader in the technology industry.

The cultural shift at IBM influenced the broader tech industry, emphasizing the importance of adaptability, innovation, and a customer-centric approach.

This real-life example demonstrates that even in a hostile work environment, a determined leader can shape company culture by emphasizing values, fostering collaboration, and aligning the organization's focus with its mission and external realities. IBM's transformation under Gerstner's leadership serves as an inspiring case of turning a struggling company into a thriving, positive workplace.

CHAPTER 11

Becoming an Advocate

Thus far, we have discussed how to navigate, report, and combat a hostile work environment. We've delved into tools for initiating organizational change and methods for influencing from within. Now, we shift focus to a role that takes your involvement to the next level—becoming an advocate for a better work environment. This chapter serves as a guide for those who wish to not just survive, but to lead the charge in transforming workplace culture.

Becoming an advocate means actively participating in or leading efforts to make your workplace more equitable and less hostile. This isn't just about remedying your situation; it's about creating a sustainable environment that allows everyone to thrive. It's about taking your personal experiences and lessons learned and using them to benefit others who may be in similar situations.

In this chapter, we will explore the pathways available for becoming an effective advocate, the challenges you may face, and the strategies you can employ to overcome them. Whether you're considering a role within your organization, thinking of joining an outside network, or even contemplating forming your own advocacy group, we'll provide you with the insights you need to take this impactful step.

By becoming an advocate, you not only create a lasting legacy but also contribute to the broader movement for workplace equity and mental well-being. Your voice and actions can serve as catalysts for change, affecting not just your immediate environment but also influencing industry standards and societal norms. So, are you ready to become an agent of change? Let's get started.

Sharing Your Story

One of the most potent tools in your advocacy toolkit is your own story. Sharing personal experiences can serve as a mirror for others who are facing similar challenges, offering them not only the validation that they are not alone but also potential pathways to navigate their own situations. In this section, we'll explore the various dimensions of sharing your story, including the platforms you can use, the impact it can have, and the precautions to take.

The Right Platform

Social Media
Social media can be a powerful avenue for sharing your story and reaching a wide audience quickly.

Blogs and Articles
Long-form content allows you to delve into the details of your experience and offer more nuanced insights.

Public Speaking and Workshops
Engaging with an audience in real-time can have a strong emotional impact and provide immediate feedback.

Crafting Your Narrative

Honesty is the Best Policy
Your story's power lies in its authenticity. Be as honest as possible about what you've been through.

Focus on Lessons Learned
While recounting experiences is crucial, the real value comes from the lessons you've learned and can share with others.

Inspire Action
End your story with actionable advice or steps that listeners or readers can take to better their own situations or become advocates themselves.

The Ripple Effect

Awareness
Your story can enlighten those unaware of the existence or extent of hostile work environments.

Empathy and Solidarity
Those who have undergone or are undergoing similar experiences may find solace and validation in your story.

Policy Influence
Powerful narratives often catch the attention of decision-makers and can contribute to policy changes within an organization.

Precautions and Ethical Considerations

Confidentiality
Ensure that you don't disclose information that can jeopardize your employment or infringe upon the privacy of others.

Emotional Well-being
Sharing your story can be emotionally draining or triggering. Make sure you're emotionally prepared and consider seeking the support of a mental health professional.

Legal Implications
Be aware of any potential legal consequences of sharing your story, especially if it involves accusations against specific individuals or organizations.

Sharing your story isn't just a therapeutic exercise; it's an act of courage that can inspire change on multiple levels—from individual attitudes to organizational policies. However, this powerful tool must be wielded responsibly and ethically to ensure its effectiveness and protect all involved parties. By sharing your experiences, you not only lend a voice to the silent but also contribute tangibly to the broader movement for a fairer, more respectful work environment.

Building a Community of Support

While individual efforts are impactful, there's unparalleled strength in numbers. Building a community of support can greatly amplify your advocacy work, providing a stronger voice and a wider reach in your quest for a healthier workplace environment. This chapter explores the ways you can build and maintain a community that backs your advocacy efforts, from identifying potential allies to creating shared platforms for discussion and action.

Identifying Allies

In the Workplace
Seek out colleagues who share your concerns and are willing to take action. They could be facing the same issues or simply be empathetic to the cause.

External Networks
Don't limit your search for allies to your immediate work environment. Industry associations, online forums, and social media can be rich sources of support.

Creating Platforms

Online Forums

Create or join existing online spaces where people can share their experiences, advice, and resources related to combating hostile work environments.

Regular Meetups
Physical or virtual meetings provide a more intimate setting for discussions and can help maintain the momentum of your advocacy efforts.

Generating Resources

Crowdfunding
Financial resources can often be a limiting factor. Platforms like GoFundMe can be useful in raising funds for specific advocacy projects or initiatives.

Expert Contributions
Solicit contributions in the form of time and expertise from professionals like employment lawyers, psychologists, and organizational development experts.

Establishing Roles and Responsibilities

Coordinators
Appoint individuals who will coordinate activities, manage communication, and ensure that goals are being met.

Committees
Create specialized committees focused on various aspects of advocacy such as policy change, outreach, and employee support.

Communication Strategies

Regular Updates
Use newsletters, social media, or group chats to keep the community informed of progress, upcoming events, and calls to action.

Feedback Mechanisms
Establish channels where community members can provide feedback, voice concerns, and contribute new ideas.

Celebrating Achievements

Acknowledge Contributions
Regularly highlight and celebrate the contributions of community members to keep morale high and encourage continued participation.

Milestone Celebrations
Acknowledge significant achievements or milestones, such as successfully influencing a policy change, through formal recognitions or celebrations.

Sustaining the Community

Ongoing Engagement
Sustain interest through continuous engagement activities like webinars, skill-building workshops, and networking events.

Succession Planning
Ensure the community's longevity by identifying and training new leaders who can take over when current

leaders step down.

Building a community of support isn't just about adding numbers to your cause; it's about creating a nurturing and empowering environment that multiplies your advocacy impact. Each community member brings unique skills, perspectives, and resources that can enrich the collective effort. Through careful planning, consistent communication, and a culture of mutual respect and acknowledgement, your community can become a formidable force in the fight against hostile work environments.

Real-Life Case: Ellen Pao's Advocacy for Workplace Equality (2015 - Present)

Ellen Pao's advocacy for workplace equality and her involvement in high-profile legal cases, including her lawsuit against a prominent Silicon Valley venture capital firm, exemplifies a real-life example of becoming an advocate against a hostile work environment.

Background:

Ellen Pao is a former partner at Kleiner Perkins Caufield & Byers, a major venture capital firm in Silicon Valley. In 2012, she filed a lawsuit against her former employer, alleging gender discrimination, retaliation, and a hostile work environment.

Becoming an Advocate:

Legal Action Against Kleiner Perkins: Ellen Pao's lawsuit against Kleiner Perkins drew attention to issues of gender bias and a hostile work environment in the male-dominated tech and venture capital industry. She claimed that she had faced discrimination, harassment, and retaliation during her tenure at the firm.

Public Awareness and Advocacy: Pao's case garnered significant media coverage, sparking conversations about gender discrimination and workplace equality in Silicon Valley and beyond. She became an advocate for diversity, inclusion, and equal treatment in the tech industry.

Founding Project Include: After her legal battle, Ellen Pao co-founded Project Include, an organization dedicated to promoting workplace diversity and inclusion in the tech sector. The organization provides guidance and resources for companies to improve their workplace cultures.

Speaking Out: Pao has used her platform to speak out against hostile work environments, discrimination, and harassment. She has become a vocal advocate for employees who face similar challenges and has encouraged others to share their stories.

Impact and Results:

While Ellen Pao's lawsuit against Kleiner Perkins did not result in a legal victory, it had a profound impact on the tech industry by shedding light on gender discrimination and the need for cultural change.

Pao's advocacy, both through legal action and her work with Project Include, has contributed to increased awareness and efforts to address issues of diversity, inclusion, and workplace equality in Silicon Valley and the broader tech community.

Her resilience and determination have inspired others to become advocates for change in their own workplaces and industries, emphasizing the importance of standing up against hostile work environments and discrimination.

Ellen Pao's journey from experiencing a hostile work environment to becoming an advocate for workplace equality exemplifies how individuals can use their experiences and platforms to drive change. Her efforts have sparked important conversations and initiatives aimed at creating more inclusive and respectful workplaces, particularly in the tech industry.

CHAPTER 12

Preparing for the Worst:
Exit Strategies

Planning Your Exit - Knowing When and How to Leave a Hostile Work Environment

While the ultimate goal is to improve your workplace, there may be situations where leaving becomes the most viable or healthy option for you. An exit is not an admission of defeat; rather, it's an act of self-preservation and sometimes even a strategic move to catalyze change from outside the organization. This chapter will guide you through the steps to thoughtfully plan your exit while ensuring that you leave on your terms.

Evaluating Your Situation

Quality of Life
If the hostile environment is affecting your mental and physical well-being, it may be time to consider an

exit.

Professional Development
Assess how the hostile environment is affecting your career growth. Is it stalling your advancement or corroding your skills?

Support System
Take stock of your support within and outside the organization. Is it sufficient to make staying worthwhile?

Pre-Exit Checklist

Update Your Resume
Ensure your resume is up to date with your latest skills, experiences, and accomplishments.

Networking
Reach out to industry contacts, attend networking events, or join online forums relevant to your field.

Financial Preparedness
Save a financial cushion to support yourself during the transition period.

Exit Strategies

Immediate Departure
In extreme situations, an immediate exit might be necessary for your well-being. Understand the legal and financial implications.

Gradual Transition
If possible, look for a new job while still employed,

making the transition smoother.

Internal Transfer
Consider if a different department within the same organization would offer a healthier environment.

Legal Considerations

Review Contracts
Examine your employment contract for any clauses that might impact your exit, such as non-compete or confidentiality agreements.

Document Everything
Continue to keep records of incidents that justify your exit. This documentation may be important for legal reasons or even for securing unemployment benefits.

The Actual Exit

Resignation Letter
Write a professional and clear resignation letter. You don't have to go into great detail about your reasons for leaving, but do keep a personal copy that might contain those details for your records.

Exit Interview
Be prepared for an exit interview. Decide in advance how candid you want to be about the reasons for your departure.

Post-Exit Actions

Farewell to Colleagues
Leave on good terms with your colleagues. They could

be valuable contacts in the future.

Reflect and Realign
Take some time post-exit to recover and reassess your career goals and personal needs.

Planning your exit from a hostile work environment requires strategic thought, financial planning, and emotional readiness. While leaving may feel like a difficult step, it can often be the first move towards a healthier, more fulfilling professional life. Know that exiting is not an end but a new beginning, offering you the opportunity to find or create a workplace where you can truly thrive.

Career Transitions and Future-Proofing

Exiting a hostile work environment can be both liberating and daunting. While you've stepped away from a harmful situation, you may also be stepping into the unknown. This section is dedicated to helping you transition into a new phase of your career while also equipping you with strategies to future-proof your professional life against similar pitfalls.

Making the Transition Smooth

Take a Breather
It's okay to take some time off between jobs to reset emotionally and physically if your financial situation allows for it.

Skill Assessment
Do a thorough evaluation of your skills, both technical

and soft, to identify what you can offer to a new role or company.

Job Search Strategy
Craft a targeted job search strategy based on your skillset, interests, and preferred company culture.

First Impressions and Early Days

Research and Reconnaissance
Before accepting a new job, do extensive research on the company culture, policies, and team dynamics, if possible.

Onboarding Wisely
During your first few weeks, be observant and ask questions to understand the workflow and office dynamics better.

Set Boundaries
Early on, establish your work-life boundaries and make your expectations clear to your team and supervisors.

Future-Proofing Strategies

Ongoing Learning
Engage in continuous learning to keep your skills relevant. This can be through courses, certifications, or webinars.

Network Building
Maintain a robust professional network inside and outside your company. These connections can be

crucial if you find yourself needing to make another transition.

Emotional Intelligence
Work on building your emotional intelligence to navigate interpersonal relationships in the workplace effectively.

Responding to Red Flags

Early Detection
Be vigilant for signs of a hostile work environment in your new job and address concerns proactively.

Back-Up Plan
Always have a contingency plan, which could include a financial safety net and an updated resume, among other things.

Support System
Maintain a reliable support system of mentors, peers, and possibly mental health professionals to consult in difficult times.

Exit Strategy 2.0

Even in your new role, understand what your exit strategy would be if things turn sour. It's not being pessimistic; it's being prepared.

Transitioning Careers

Changing Fields
If your experience has soured your interest in your current field, consider transitioning to another.

Assess what skills are transferable and what additional training you might need.

Freelancing or Entrepreneurship
If traditional employment isn't appealing, consider freelancing or starting your own business.

Transitions are never easy, but they offer new beginnings. By approaching your next career move with intention and foresight, you can not only make the transition smoother but also set yourself up for long-term success. Future-proofing your career involves a mix of skill development, emotional intelligence, and prudent planning. Equipped with these tools, you'll be better prepared to thrive in any work environment that comes your way.

Real-Life Case: Whitney Wolfe Herd's Exit from Tinder and Founding Bumble (2014)

Whitney Wolfe Herd's experience at Tinder and her subsequent exit to found Bumble is a real-life example of preparing for the worst, including an exit strategy, in a hostile work environment. Her journey highlights how individuals can respond to adversity and turn challenging situations into opportunities for personal and professional growth.

Background:

Whitney Wolfe Herd was one of the co-founders of Tinder, a popular dating app, and served as its Vice President of Marketing. However, her time at Tinder became increasingly challenging due to a hostile work environment and personal harassment.

Preparing for the Worst: Exit Strategies:

Hostile Work Environment at Tinder: Whitney Wolfe Herd faced a hostile work environment at Tinder, including alleged discrimination and mistreatment. She filed a lawsuit against the company and her co-founders, accusing them of sexual harassment and discrimination.

Exit and Founding Bumble: As part of the settlement of her lawsuit, Wolfe Herd left Tinder. However, instead of retreating from the tech industry, she used her experience to prepare for the worst and launch her own dating app, Bumble, with a focus on empowering women in online dating.

Bumble's Success: Bumble quickly gained popularity for its unique approach, which allowed women to make the first move in conversations, giving them more control and reducing harassment. The app became a significant competitor to Tinder.

Impact and Results:

Whitney Wolfe Herd's exit from Tinder and founding of Bumble not only allowed her to escape a hostile work environment but also empowered her to create a platform that prioritized safety, respect, and gender equality in online dating.

Bumble's success as a business, coupled with its

commitment to addressing issues of harassment and discrimination, set an example for the tech industry and inspired other entrepreneurs to prioritize inclusivity and safety in their own ventures.

Wolfe Herd's journey showcases how an exit strategy can be a powerful tool in responding to a hostile work environment. Instead of being defined by her negative experiences, she used them as motivation to create positive change in the industry.

This real-life example demonstrates how preparing for the worst and having an exit strategy can lead to unexpected opportunities and personal growth. Whitney Wolfe Herd's decision to exit a hostile work environment and found Bumble not only transformed her own career but also contributed to positive changes in the online dating industry.

CONCLUSION

A Final Word: Thriving,
Not Just Surviving

As we come to the end of this comprehensive guide on navigating hostile work environments, the ultimate message is clear: the goal is not merely to survive, but to thrive. While survival tactics are essential in adverse circumstances, they are stepping stones to a greater objective. The aim is to cultivate an environment where you, and ideally everyone around you, can achieve personal and professional growth without fear or compromise.

A Paradigm Shift

Survival is about resilience in the face of adversity; it's about weathering the storm. Thriving, however, implies a paradigm shift. It suggests an environment where you're not just resilient but actually flourish.

The tools and strategies outlined in this book are designed to help you effect this paradigm shift, either by transforming your current work environment or by equipping you to find or create a healthier one.

Collective Efforts

Although this guide has been heavily focused on individual actions, the transformative power of collective efforts can't be overstated. An environment where everyone thrives is the collective responsibility of the entire workforce, from entry-level employees to top-level management. Advocate for change not just for yourself, but also for those around you who might not have the resources, courage, or platform to speak up.

Onward and Upward

Leaving a hostile work environment is not the end of the journey but a milestone. Use the lessons learned as building blocks for a brighter future. Each experience, good or bad, contributes to your overall growth and understanding of what you need to truly thrive in your career.

Your Story Matters

Lastly, don't underestimate the power of sharing your story, whether it's one of triumph or ongoing struggle. Your insights could be the lifeline someone else needs to navigate their own hostile work environment. Moreover, it contributes to the broader dialogue on workplace culture, ultimately pushing organizations toward creating healthier environments.

You are not alone, and you don't have to settle for merely surviving. With the right tools, support, and mindset, thriving is within your reach. While the journey may be difficult and fraught with challenges, the destination—a fulfilling and enriching work life— is worth every effort.

Thank you for walking this path with us. Here's to your future, one where you don't merely survive, but truly thrive.

Tools and Resources for Ongoing Support

The journey through a hostile work environment can often feel lonely, but you don't have to navigate it in isolation. This final chapter provides a roundup of resources and tools designed to offer ongoing support as you aim to not just survive, but thrive in your work life.

Books and Literature

Self-Help Books

"Daring Greatly" by Brené Brown
"Crucial Conversations" by Al Switzler, Joseph Grenny, and Ron McMillan

Academic Journals

"Journal of Occupational Health Psychology"
"Journal of Vocational Behavior"

These resources offer both actionable advice and theoretical background to help you understand workplace dynamics better.

Online Platforms

Websites

- ✓ Glassdoor for company reviews
- ✓ MindTools for skill development resources

Blogs and Newsletters

- ✓ Harvard Business Review's sections on Leadership and Organizational Culture
- ✓ Work Awesome's blogs on workplace issues

Stay updated on workplace trends and get expert advice at your fingertips.

Support Groups

Online Forums

- ✓ Reddit's r/work and r/jobs
- ✓ Workplace Stack Exchange

Physical Groups

- ✓ Local industry-specific networking events
- ✓ Employee assistance programs

Use these platforms for real-life advice, experience sharing, and emotional support.

Professional Services

Legal Advice

- ✓ Avvo
- ✓ American Bar Association's lawyer search

Mental Health Services

- ✓ BetterHelp for online therapy
- ✓ Psychology Today's therapist finder for in-person support

Consult professionals for specialized advice and support.

Apps and Software

Stress Management

- ✓ Headspace for guided meditation
- ✓ MyLife Meditation for stress reduction and emotional check-ins

Record-Keeping

- ✓ Evernote for documenting incidents
- ✓ Google Drive for securely storing documentation

These tools can help you maintain your well-being and keep vital records.

Webinars and Courses

Soft Skills Development

- ✓ LinkedIn Learning
- ✓ Udemy's Workplace Behavior courses

Leadership and Advocacy Training

✓ Coursera's organizational culture classes
✓ Harvard's online Leadership, Organizing and Action course

Improve your skills and become an advocate for change.

Company-Specific Resources

Don't ignore the resources available within your organization, such as:

✓ Human Resources support
✓ In-house training and workshops
✓ Employee assistance programs (EAP)

Thriving in a hostile work environment is an ongoing process that requires constant vigilance and adaptability. Fortunately, you don't have to go it alone. Utilize these tools and resources to arm yourself with the knowledge, skills, and support network you need to turn your professional life around. Remember, the objective is not just to endure, but to flourish—and these resources can help you do just that.

APPENDICES

Sample Documentation Templates

Documentation is a crucial aspect of dealing with a hostile work environment, and it's essential to keep records that are clear, detailed, and professional. Here are some sample templates to guide you in documenting various workplace incidents.

Incident Report Template

General Information
- Date of Incident:
- Time of Incident:
- Location of Incident:

Involved Parties
- Your Name:
- Title/Position:

Department:

Name of Person(s) Involved:

Title/Position:

Department:

Detailed Description of Incident

Provide a comprehensive description of the incident, including:

- What happened?
- What led up to the event?
- Were there any witnesses? (Provide their names and contact details, if available.)

Attachments

Include any additional material that supports your case:

- Emails
- Text Messages
- Photos
- Videos

Action Taken

- Did you report the incident? (Yes/No)
- If yes, to whom?
- What was their response?

Harassment/Bullying Complaint Template

General Information

- Date of Complaint:

- Name of Complainant:
- Name of Accused:

Specifics of the Complaint

Describe the harassment or bullying in detail:

- Type of harassment/bullying (verbal, physical, cyber)
- Frequency and duration
- How it has affected your work

Witnesses and Evidence

List any witnesses and attach evidence like screenshots, emails, or other documentation.

Desired Outcome

What do you hope to achieve by filing this complaint?

<u>Meeting Summary Template</u>

After you've had a meeting about a workplace issue, it's helpful to have a written record.

General Information

- Date of Meeting:
- Attendees:

Key Points Discussed

Briefly summarize the main topics covered.

Actions Agreed Upon

What are the next steps?

Additional Notes

Any other observations or things to remember.

Note: Always store these documents securely, both electronically and physically, and consider sharing them with a trusted individual outside your workplace for additional safekeeping.

These templates are starting points and can be adapted to fit the specifics of your situation. Use them to maintain consistent, accurate records that can be vital for resolving issues effectively.

List of Resources and Support Organizations

Emotional and Psychological Support

BetterHelp - Online counseling and therapy services.
Website: BetterHelp

Psychology Today - Find local therapists and counselors.
Website: Psychology Today

Employee Assistance Programs (EAP) - Check if

your organization offers an EAP for free counseling services.

Legal Support

Avvo - Free legal advice and lawyer directory.
Website: Avvo

American Bar Association - Legal resources and lawyer search.
Website: ABA (Or the Bar Association of your country)

LegalAdvice Subreddit - Get preliminary legal advice.
Website: r/legaladvice

Workplace Rights and Policy Organizations

U.S. Equal Employment Opportunity Commission (EEOC)
Website: EEOC

ACAS (Advisory, Conciliation and Arbitration Service) for UK
Website: ACAS

Fair Work Ombudsman for Australia
Website: Fair Work

Or any similar organization in your state or country.

Forums and Online Communities

Reddit's Work and Jobs Forums

r/work
r/jobs

Workplace Stack Exchange
Website: Workplace SE

Glassdoor
Company reviews and workplace culture assessments.
Website: Glassdoor

Educational Resources

LinkedIn Learning
Online courses on soft skills, workplace behavior, and leadership.
Website: LinkedIn Learning

Udemy
Online courses on various professional skills.
Website: Udemy

Coursera
Academic courses on organizational culture and human resources.
Website: Coursera

Support Groups and Networking

Meetup
Local and virtual meetups for professional networking and support.
Website: Meetup

Industry-Specific Associations
Look for organizations and associations in your industry that offer networking events and resources.

Toastmasters
Improve your public speaking and leadership skills. Website: Toastmasters

These resources can offer different types of support, from emotional well-being to legal aid. Remember, you're not alone on your journey through a hostile work environment, and these organizations and resources can be invaluable allies.

Frequently Asked Questions

General Questions

1. What constitutes a hostile work environment?

A hostile work environment is created when an individual experiences behavior, actions, or language that is discriminatory, abusive, or intimidating, making it difficult for them to perform their job duties effectively.

2. How can I identify if my workplace is hostile?

Signs of a hostile work environment include consistent negative behavior directed towards you or others, unjust criticism, exclusion, derogatory language, or any form of harassment or discrimination.

3. Is a one-time incident enough to label a workplace as hostile?

Typically, isolated incidents are not enough to constitute a hostile work environment unless they are extremely severe or dangerous. A pattern of behavior over time is usually required for legal action.

Reporting and Documentation

4. To whom should I report incidents in a hostile work environment?

Initial reports should generally be made to your immediate supervisor or the human resources department. If the issue involves these parties, you may need to consult your company's reporting hierarchy or use an anonymous reporting mechanism if available.

5. What should I document in case of an incident?

Details like date, time, location, involved parties, and a comprehensive description of the incident should be documented. Any available evidence such as emails, text messages, or witness statements should also be included.

Legal and Organizational Questions

6. What are the legal remedies available for dealing with a hostile work environment?

Legal options may include filing a formal complaint with agencies like the EEOC in the U.S., or equivalent organizations in other countries. Lawsuits may also be an option, depending on the severity and impact of the conduct.

7. Does the law protect me from retaliation?

Yes, laws like Title VII of the Civil Rights Act in the U.S. protect employees from retaliation for reporting harassment or discrimination. Similar protections exist in other jurisdictions.

Emotional and Psychological Well-being

8. How can I manage stress in a hostile work environment?

Strategies include engaging in mindfulness techniques, exercise, professional counseling, and utilizing employee assistance programs if available.

9. Can a hostile work environment affect my health?

Yes, prolonged exposure to a hostile work environment can lead to stress, anxiety, depression, and other physical and mental health issues.

Company Culture and Advocacy

10. Can I influence the culture in my workplace to be less hostile?

Yes, although it can be challenging. You can aim to influence from within by setting a positive example, sharing constructive feedback, and engaging in advocacy and education efforts.

11. What if nothing changes after reporting?

If you've exhausted all internal avenues for resolution with no improvement, you may need to consider external options like legal action or finding a new job.

These FAQs are designed to provide a general overview of the issues surrounding hostile work environments. For personalized advice, consult professionals in legal, psychological, and human resources fields.

Thank you for taking the time to read to the end of this book. It is my hope that by now, you should have a comprehensive understanding of what a hostile work environment is, how to cope with it, and how to either enact change or make the decision to leave for a better opportunity.

EPILOGUE

*A Journey Towards
Empowerment and Change*

As we conclude this comprehensive guide on "Thriving in a Hostile Work Environment," it's essential to reflect on the journey you've embarked upon. We've explored the complexities of hostile work environments, from recognizing the signs to taking decisive actions and advocating for change. Your journey through these pages has been a testament to your resilience and determination.

The stories of those who have persevered in the face of adversity and the strategies you've learned to overcome workplace challenges are not just words on a page; they are blueprints for empowerment. We hope that this guide has not only armed you with knowledge but has also instilled a sense of confidence and hope.

The Power of Knowledge

Knowledge is a powerful tool, and by understanding the dynamics of hostile work environments, you have taken the first step towards creating positive change. You are now better equipped to recognize the signs, protect your rights, and support your colleagues. Informed employees can challenge unjust systems and work toward more inclusive and respectful workplaces.

Taking Action

Throughout this journey, you've learned that taking action is essential. Whether it's documenting incidents, reporting misconduct, or advocating for yourself and others, your actions can spark transformation. By raising your voice, you become an agent of change, not just for yourself but for future generations of employees.

The Impact of Support

Remember the importance of your support system, from trusted colleagues and mentors to friends and family. No one should have to navigate a hostile work environment alone. Lean on your network for emotional support, guidance, and strength.

Shaping the Future

The workplace of the future depends on individuals like you who refuse to accept hostility as the status quo. By influencing company culture, challenging discriminatory practices, and advocating for inclusive policies, you have the power to shape a brighter future for all employees.

Never Stop Thriving

As you move forward, keep in mind that thriving is not just a destination but an ongoing journey. You have the resilience to face whatever challenges come your way, and the knowledge to navigate them effectively. Never settle for mere survival when you have the potential to thrive.

Your Story Matters

Your story, like those shared throughout this guide, is part of a broader narrative of change. By sharing your experiences, you contribute to a collective voice that demands fairness, respect, and equality in the workplace. Your story matters, and it can inspire and empower others to take action.

In closing, remember that your journey is not solitary; it's part of a broader movement towards more equitable and inclusive workplaces worldwide. By thriving in a hostile work environment, you're not just changing your life—you're helping to change the world. Thank you for embarking on this journey with us, and here's to a future where everyone can truly thrive.

ACKNOWLEDGEMENT

Writing a book is a journey, and not one that can be embarked upon alone. I am deeply grateful to the individuals and organizations who have supported and inspired me through this process.

First and formost, I will like to express my appreciation to all those who have experienced and endured hostile work environment. Your stories, resilience and determination to make positive changes have been a driving force behind this book.

I want to extend my heartfelt thanks to my family and friends for their unwavering encouragement and understanding during the long hours and late nights of writing and research. Your belief in this project has meant the world to me.

To the countless experts, professionals and advocates who generously shared their knowledge and insight, thank you for your invaluable contributions. Your expertise has added depth and credibility to these pages.

I'd also like to acknowledge the team at Vista Press for their guidance, patience and dedication to bringing this book to life.

Lastly, to the readers, I'm humbled and grateful that you have chosen to explore this topic with me. It is my sincere hope that the information within these pages will empower you to navigate and ultimately thrive in any challenging work environment you may encounter.

Thank you all for being part of this important journey.

With gratitude.

Victor Olewunne MPE

ABOUT THE AUTHOR

Victor Olewunne

Victor Olewunne is the Chief Consultant at Protarget Communications Limited. He has been in the marketing communication profession for over 30 years. Yes, 30 years of research, business consultancy and marketing communication challenges. Since compassion and  empathy is at the core of his person, he has learnt to dig deep, filter out the noises and analytically identify what the real life's problems are. That done, the solution he proffers become fun that turns everything around for good.

His experience as a life and business coach has taught him that there are more perceived problems than real ones. With the right information and tools, no problem is worth a sleepless night.Through his entrepreneurship journey, starting and running several businesses over the years, he has come across and surmounted most of the challenges of life and business.

His life's focus now is to extend his experience, researched and proven solutions to all those who may be at one of the cross roads of life.He is here to hold your hand to a life of powerful information and solutions.

Victor Olewunne. BA. MPE (Masters in Professional Ethics)"

BOOKS BY THIS AUTHOR

Don't Marry The Right Person

A Twist in the Tale

In a world brimming with love stories that promise happily ever afters, let us embark on a journey that challenges the conventional wisdom of finding the "right" person. Welcome to a realm where imperfections are celebrated, growth is cherished, and authenticity reigns supreme.

Picture this: a tapestry of relationships, each thread woven with unique patterns and shades. As we unfold these pages, let us explore a truth often whispered in hushed tones – that the pursuit of the "right" person might lead us astray from the path of genuine connection.

In these chapters, we'll navigate through the maze of compatibility and chemistry, shared values and growth, resilience through challenges, and the dance of vulnerability and communication. We'll shed light on the myths of perfection, guiding you towards embracing the beauty of imperfections and the rich depths they hold.

Imagine this book as a lantern guiding you through the uncharted territory of the heart. It's a treasure trove of insights, stories, and wisdom from the shores of experience, aimed at helping you navigate the seas of love with a compass of authenticity and a map of growth.

So, dear reader, consider this your invitation to explore a new narrative – one that celebrates the journey of partnership, the warmth of shared laughter, and the wisdom in choosing depth over superficiality. Let us embark on this adventure together, daring to question the norms and unraveling the threads of what it truly means to build a lasting, fulfilling, and wonderfully imperfect love story.

The chapters include the following:

Rethinking "The One"
The Myth of Perfect Compatibility
Embracing Imperfections: The Real Partner
Shared Values and Goals: A Strong Foundation
Resilience Through Challenges
Communication and Vulnerability
Growth Together: The Journey of Marriage

Ethics: That Guarantees And Accelerates Your Success

"Ethics is knowing the difference between what you have a right to do and what is right to do"
- Potter Steward.

In a world fueled by ambition and aspiration, the pursuit of success often takes center stage. We are drawn to stories of remarkable achievement, captivated by the journeys of those who have triumphed against all odds. Yet, in the relentless pursuit of success, an essential facet often goes overlooked—the role of ethics.

Welcome to a journey that transcends traditional notions of success. This book, "Ethics: That Guarantees and Accelerates Your Success," beckons you to explore the profound interplay between ethical principles and the attainment of true, sustainable success. Beyond the ordinary realm of achievements and accolades lies a profound truth: success is not merely about reaching a destination; it's about how you get there.

In these pages, we delve into the heart of ethics and its transformative power. From the boardrooms of corporations to the chambers of personal growth, ethics emerges as the bedrock upon which extraordinary success is built. It is not merely a set of guidelines but a philosophy that shapes decisions, relationships, and the very essence of one's character. Our exploration will navigate the intricate pathways of integrity, transparency, empathy, and responsibility. We will uncover the wisdom of ethical decision-making and the art of fostering authentic connections. We will learn how ethical leadership inspires collective growth and how the digital age challenges us to uphold moral values in new realms.

As you embark on this journey, be prepared to embark on a transformational voyage—a journey that challenges the conventional and empowers you to rise above the ordinary. Each chapter is a gateway to unlocking the secrets of ethical success, revealing the principles that not only guarantee but accelerate your ascent to greatness.

Through real-world examples, timeless philosophies, and actionable insights, you will discover that success achieved through ethics is not a mirage but a tangible reality. Whether you're a business leader aiming to steer your organization with purpose, an individual seeking personal growth with integrity, or an aspiring entrepreneur navigating uncharted waters, this book offers a guiding light.

Let us embark on this exploration with an open heart and a curious mind. Let us uncover the ways in which

ethics becomes the compass that guides us toward our dreams, and the guiding star that ensures we reach the right destination—triumphant, fulfilled, and honorable.
The journey begins now, as we set sail on the seas of ethical success.

Unplugged: Navigating The Social Media Minefield And Reclaiming Your Productivity

In a world that thrives on constant connection and instantaneous information, we find ourselves navigating the intricate landscape of social media – a realm where likes, comments, and shares shape our perceptions of ourselves and the world around us. The allure of digital platforms promises connection, inspiration, and a window into the lives of others, yet beneath the surface lies a complex minefield of distractions, comparisons, and a growing sense of detachment from the present moment.

As the digital age advances, we stand at a pivotal moment where our ability to harness the benefits of social media while mitigating its challenges becomes paramount. In this book, "Unplugged: Navigating the Social Media Minefield and Reclaiming Your Productivity," we embark on a journey to explore the multifaceted dimensions of social media's impact on our lives and the strategies that empower us to regain control over our time, attention, and productivity.

Through the pages that follow, we delve into the psychology behind social media addiction, the consequences of constant interruptions on our work and relationships, and the profound effects of the fear of missing out (FOMO) on our well-being. We dissect the mechanisms of information overload, echo chambers, and the social comparison trap, while providing actionable steps to cultivate critical thinking, mindfulness, and a balanced digital presence.

This book serves as a compass, guiding you through the twists and turns of the digital landscape, helping you navigate the minefield of distractions, and offering insights to reclaim the productivity that modern life often robs from us. It is a testament to the idea that unplugging from the noise of social media doesn't mean disconnection from the world – it's an invitation to reconnect with the richness of your own thoughts, experiences, and the authentic relationships that nourish your soul.

As you embark on this journey, may the pages ahead inspire you to challenge the status quo, to embrace intentional living in the digital age, and to embark on a path that leads to not only reclaiming your productivity but also rediscovering the profound joys that lie beyond the digital realm. Welcome to "Unplugged," where the journey to a more purposeful and connected life begins.

The target audience for this book
The target audience for this book titled "Unplugged: Navigating the Social Media Minefield and Reclaiming Productivity" generally includes individuals who are seeking to improve their focus, productivity, and well-being by managing their social media usage. Here are some specific groups that fall among the primary target audience for the book:

Young Adults and Professionals
Students
Parents
Entrepreneurs and Business Owners
Teachers and Educators
Health and Well-being Enthusiasts
Tech Professionals

Individuals Struggling with Digital Addiction: People who recognize that they have developed an addiction to social media and are actively seeking help to overcome it.

Attempts have been made to align the book's content and tone to resonate with the specific needs and concerns of the target audience. By addressing the challenges and offering practical solutions relevant to the reader's situation, the book aims to attract and benefit its intended audience.

Your Tyre Or Your Life.

This book is the first in the V-Star Motoring Series books aimed at helping motorists everywhere have a deeper understanding of some issues concerning their vehicles, which they may have hitherto been taken for granted, but which have far reaching implication on their safety, their comfort and the cost of running their car.

While safety is paramount in the purpose of this book, we are also conscious of the fact that uncontrolled economic waste and extended period of discomfort can have adverse effect on the quality of our lives. V-Star Motoring Series therefore attempts to raise the level of awareness about these issues.

Most of the information highlighted in theses series is so subtle that an average motorist can drive for many years without being aware of them. Unfortunately, not knowing does not mean not paying. We bear the cost, emotionally, psychologically or financially whether we are conscious of the facts or not. This is what makes it particularly dangerous for us all.

This volume titled, Your Tyre or Your Life, focuses on the only contact our vehicles have with mother earth, the tyres. Often overlooked, when casual glance shows us it is not flat, but it is the most critical part of any road vehicle. Since the entire weight of the vehicle rest on it, our lives practically depends on it while in the vehicle. Much attention have not been given to the issue of the use of right tyre size because more than 98% of vehicle owners get it right by simply replacing old tyres with the same specification of tyre. Though it must be stated here that an average vehicle tyre has a service life of four years. This is not how long it takes to wear out the tyre, but the period of time it takes for the rubber content of the tyre to break down beyond safe level.If you value your safety in any road vehicle, you cannot afford to ignore the tyres, particularly the air pressure in the tyres.

As the book go on the point out, the tyre air pressure, which most motorist do not check for several weeks or even months, can be life threatening, beyond undermining the quality of your driving experience and the quality of your life.This book advocates and encourages conscious effort on the part of every motorist to continually check and maintain the manufacturer recommended air pressure in the vehicle tyres at all times, for your safety and the safety of your family.Other coming titles under the series include; How to Drive Safely in Any Environment; How to Drive an Old Car Safely, Economically and in Comfort.

Opportunity Unleashed: The Ultimate Guide To Discovering, Creating And Maximising Success

"Opportunity Unleashed" is a transformative guide that illuminates the path to success by empowering readers to harness the full potential of opportunities in every aspect of their lives. This comprehensive book takes readers on a journey of self-discovery, creative thinking, and strategic planning to seize opportunities and turn them into remarkable achievements. From business ventures to personal growth, this guide equips readers with the mindset, skills, and actionable steps needed to unleash their true potential and create a life of fulfillment and success.

"Opportunity Unleashed" is a definitive guide that empowers readers to recognize, create, and maximize opportunities to achieve extraordinary success. This book is a call to action for those seeking to break free from self-imposed limitations and unlock their full potential to lead a fulfilling and purposeful life. With practical insights, simplified steps and inspiring stories, readers will be equipped to seize opportunities, embrace challenges, and unleash the power of their potential to make a lasting impact on the world.

Mothers Work-Life Balance

Welcome to "Mothers, Work-Life Balance," a book dedicated to exploring, analyzing, and illuminating one of the most discussed yet enigmatic aspects of modern life. If you've picked up this book, chances are you are a mother striving to balance your professional career with your role as a caregiver, or perhaps you're someone who is keenly interested in understanding the dynamics that affect countless mothers globally.

Being a mother is often likened to a full-time job, and that description is neither hyperbole nor understatement. The complexities of nurturing a child, managing a household, and balancing personal aspirations and goals are monumental tasks in their own right. Add a professional career to the equation, and the daily life of a working mother becomes an intricate ballet of schedules, responsibilities, and emotional labor.

Yet, despite the challenges, millions of women around the world juggle these dual roles with admirable finesse, albeit not without sacrifices. In a society that glorifies "having it all," there's an unspoken sentiment that somehow, women should be able to effortlessly blend these roles into a seamless life. But can mothers truly "have it all" in the way society often suggests? Is the concept of work-life balance a realistic goal or a societal myth that sets women up for failure—or perhaps somewhere in between?

This book aims to deconstruct the many layers of this topic, presenting a multi-dimensional understanding of the challenges and opportunities that come with balancing motherhood and professional life. Divided into five parts, we will delve into societal myths, workplace dynamics, the home front, self-care, and practical strategies for achieving a sense of equilibrium.

In Part I, we'll explore the societal frameworks that shape our understanding of motherhood and career, focusing on how culture and economics create unique pressures for women.

Part II will examine the professional landscape, discussing the policies, environments, and attitudes that either aid or hinder a mother's journey towards balance.

In Part III, we'll shift our focus to the home, exploring how familial roles, relationships, and domestic responsibilities can be managed effectively.

Part IV is a comprehensive guide to self-care, highlighting why taking care of yourself is not selfish but essential for both your well-being and the happiness of your family.

Lastly, Part V will offer actionable advice, providing you with tools and strategies to approach your dual roles with more confidence and less stress.

Through a blend of research, interviews, case studies, and personal insights, this book aims to be both a theoretical exploration and a practical guide. We'll hear from mothers from various walks of life—entrepreneurs, hourly workers, freelancers, and executives, among others—allowing us to examine the issue of work-life balance through multiple lenses. The journey towards balance is neither straightforward nor the same for every mother. Yet, the quest is universal. Let's embark on this journey together, breaking down barriers, questioning norms, and, most importantly, seeking balance in the beautiful chaos that is motherhood.

So, are you ready to redefine what balance means to you? Let's begin.
Thank you for embarking on this journey with us. We hope that by the end, you'll be better equipped to tackle the intricate jigsaw puzzle that is a mother's life, piecing together a picture that, while not perfect, is profoundly and uniquely yours.

Deontological Examination Of The Ethics Of The Knowledge Economy

This study is prompted by the need to enquire to what extent the world that has been aware and enamored with the metaphysics of Immanuel Kant's deontological ethics has applied the same in the conducts that gave rise to the phenomenon generally known today as globalization or knowledge economy. Saddled with many negative impacts worldwide, it questions the place of altruism in human actions.

Following Kant's assertions that humans are autonomous reasoning beings, it x-rays the dissonance between the realities and the position of the neo-capitalist liberalist in the human exercise of free choices. Identifying the essential ingredients of deontology delineates its strengths and shortcomings and points towards alternative metaphysical considerations in evaluating and dealing with dilemmas emanating from globalization.

It proffers that deontological ethics can be reprogrammed to adopt a more global approach in policy formulation and implementations to address the many issues ensuing from globalization. However, as a principle based on western philosophy anchored on individualism, it is limited in scope to solve the problems it has created. African theory of complementary ethics based on African philosophy of communality and relationship is presented to provide a viable approach to dealing with the many issues and problems globalization has trumped up in this era of knowledge economy. This is more critical now that speed and intensity of interdependence and global impact needs to be matched by humanistic elements for all humanity to thrive.

Keywords: Deontology, ethics, globalization, altruism, knowledge economy, African philosophy, communalism, relationship.

Philosophies For Self-Fulfilment

A Journey of Self-Fulfillment
In the tapestry of human existence, the quest for self-fulfillment has been a timeless pursuit, an exploration that transcends cultures, eras, and philosophies. This

book is an invitation to embark on a profound journey —a journey within oneself, through diverse philosophical landscapes, and towards a life enriched with purpose, wisdom, and inner harmony.

In an ever-changing world, where the cacophony of external influences often drowns the whispers of our inner desires, the need to reconnect with our true selves has never been more vital. Philosophies for self-fulfillment offer guiding stars, illuminating pathways to understanding, growth, and the realization of our fullest potential.

As we delve into the pages that follow, we will encounter an array of philosophies, both ancient and contemporary, each offering a unique lens through which we can view our lives. We will explore Stoicism's call to embrace adversity with unwavering resilience, African philosophy's celebration of interconnectedness and communal well-being, the art of mindfulness that anchors us in the present moment, the pursuit of meaning that infuses our actions with purpose, and the cultivation of gratitude that transforms our outlook on the world.

Amidst these philosophies, you will find, not only the wisdom of great thinkers but also practical exercises, real-life anecdotes, and tangible examples that bridge the gap between theory and daily living. From the stoic sailor navigating treacherous waters to the grateful farmer celebrating unity in scarcity, these stories illuminate the potential for profound transformation and fulfillment when philosophy intertwines with lived experience.

With each turn of the page, we invite you to reflect, to introspect, and to engage. The chapters that follow offer a roadmap, a compass, and a mirror, guiding you through the landscapes of your own thoughts, emotions, and actions. They beckon you to explore the inner recesses of your being, to examine your relationships with the world around you, and to uncover the gems of wisdom that lie within.

This is a book of exploration, an exploration of self, of diverse philosophies, and of the intricate tapestry that binds them. It is an exploration that acknowledges that the journey toward self-fulfillment is not a solitary endeavor; it is a journey that we undertake together, drawing strength and inspiration from the shared experiences of humanity.

As you embark on this journey, may you find inspiration, guidance, and a renewed sense of purpose. May you be encouraged to seek deeper connections, both within yourself and with the world around you. May you discover that the pursuit of self-fulfillment is not a destination, but a lifelong expedition—a voyage that enriches not only your life but the lives of those you touch.

Welcome to "Philosophies for Self-Fulfillment," where the pages are an open invitation to explore, learn, and transform.

Discover Your Child's Talent, For Early Success In Life.

How do I discover, no, identify the natural talents of my child so I can focus on helping the child develop along that line of giftedness.

This book is a thoroughly researched compilation of guides and steps that will help all parents to understand their children, learn how to observe, and identify those critical flashes of genius indicative of special abilities in your child. It further tells how you can support and nurture the abilities to early maturity, making life and learning fun for the child and peace of mind for the parents.

Financially, this saves you loads because there won't be any investment in areas that do not interest the child. You eliminate the possibility of post-school career dilemma or mid-age career crisis which a lot of people go through. With this right foundation, every other thing will be an extension of or new trajectories of a well-grounded pursuit and calling.
What better can parents do for their children than this, none if you ask me.

Download a copy of this book and be empowered to make the right decisions and make the right investment for your child's development, growth, and early success in life.

Love and responsibility made me put this together, only LOVE AND RESPONSIBILITY will make any parent quickly get this vital compilation for their children.

32 Easy Steps To Make Your Child Top The Class.

This Special book is a carefully researched document on what makes the top students outperform all others. It is a sure key to making your child top the class. It starts with a case study of Asian and American students, then it reveals a process that gives very consistent results

It will make you want to apologize to the child for all the abuse and blames you have been piling on him or her. It will reset your mind about the awesome gifts and abilities of your child. It will put you firmly in the driver's seat while your child reaps the benefit, and you can take the glory.

This book brings to the fore many little things you have been neglecting or taking for granted which makes a huge impact on your child's academic performance.

Following the steps laid out in this book, completely reprograms you and your child for success, not only in academics but in life generally. It is a negligible investment compared to what you dole out to the schools every term.